MARRIED TO MOM

MARRIED TO MOM

LEARNING TO RECOGNIZE HIDDEN
RED FLAGS IN A RELATIONSHIP
WITH A MOTHER-ENMESHED
COVERT NARCISSIST

MICHAELA BRESSEL

NEW DEGREE PRESS

MARRIED TO MOM

Learning to Recognize Hidden Red Flags in a Relationship with a Mother-Enmeshed Covert Narcissist

ISBN   978-1-63730-332-0   *Paperback*

978-1-63730-333-7   *Kindle Ebook*

978-1-63730-334-4   *Ebook*

Dedication

To a very special person.
YOU.

In memory of my husband, Lester.
Forever in my heart.

TABLE OF CONTENTS

———

"In his unconscious—and sometimes conscious—mind, a mother-enmeshed man is representing his mother's interests, while his own have become secondary."

—DR. KENNETH M. ADAMS

INTRODUCTION

Dear readers,

I have always been told that I should marry a man who loves his mother. Finally, in my early fifties, I find myself at a cross-roads with that theory as I am grieving the loss of my husband. He not only seemed to have loved his mother so much that he wasn't able to ever fully commit himself to any other woman, but in the end died from a heart attack at the young age of forty-six due to lifelong emotional distress, anxiety, and consequential health issues like high blood pressure, being overweight, and coronary artery disease.

This book is for you if you are or are with someone who loves their mom and has thoughts like …

"Growing up, it felt like I took the role of my dad."

"I always wonder if Mom is okay with it. Always."

"I grew up feeling responsible for my mom."

"I love my mom, but I feel like I can't even breathe without her approval."

"Sometimes I feel more like a mistress than a wife."

"His mom is just too involved in our marriage."

"I will never measure up to his mom."

"He consults his mom but won't tell me about it."

You are not alone in the way you feel. There's such a thing as an unhealthy level of motherly love. The questions you may have, the doubts, the feeling that you're crazy and making things up are valid. They might be the result of the silent emotional abuse you may have endured. The damage done is likely in your internal world, invisible to your friends and family that may not seem to understand or may make you feel like you are blowing things out of proportion. Reading this book may help you to identify if the parent-child relationship you're dealing with is of a healthy nature. You may also find answers to questions you don't even know you have.

I met my husband Lester a little over eight years ago. Everything about him was perfect. We were perfect. We called ourselves soulmates, while others called us "the cute couple." He was a kind and caring man, quiet and well-mannered in appearance, and had a close relationship with his mom. At first, I adored him for taking care of her for all his adult life. It seemed he was treating me with the same love and respect he had for her. He spoiled me from the very beginning and made all my dreams come true.

But after just a few months of dating, his love for his mother kept interfering with our love as a couple. Then later, it had an ever-growing negative effect on our marriage. Our love story quickly became an emotional roller coaster with extreme highs and lows. It was a mix of a perfect marriage and emotional breakdowns, mainly concerning his constant lies that I excused and forgave each and every time, blaming his mother as the root of all evil.

My explanation was that she was a hateful and unhappy lady who had a bit too much control over her son, and he did whatever it took to please her. I saw my husband as the victim, the son that was raised by an egocentric, hateful, coldhearted woman. I was on a mission to show him how beautiful love was supposed to feel.

Two and a half years into our relationship, Lester got into a very bad car accident. This became a turning point in our marriage and truly turned out to be the beginning of the end. His mother's behavior toward me became extremely hostile and unnaturally possessive over her son. It was at that time that a friend suggested my mother-in-law was a narcissist and that my husband was emotionally damaged. This advice triggered a chain reaction that led me to years of research. I read books, watched YouTube videos, and googled anything I could find about the subject of narcissism. I was shocked to learn that she fit the traits so very well. At that point, I still excused his behavior and attributed it to him being raised by a narcissistic mother, never even thinking that he too could be a narcissist of some form.

Another five years later, halfway through 2020, I finally found myself emotionally worn out, empty, and clueless. I was left wondering if our marital issues were all because of his upbringing or because I was making excuses for things like the lies he told and the secrets he kept. I wanted to find out if his mother was the person that destroyed our marriage or if there was something else that caused our relationship to fall apart.

How could my husband's love for his mom seem so perfect at first but end up destroying our marriage?

Why did it leave me feeling overly sensitive, overly reactive, and thinking I'm selfish and controlling?

Was I wrong to hope he would learn to appreciate and love me in a different way than the dysfunctional attachment he shared with his mother?

I came to the conclusion there had to be more to the way he acted and the way it made me feel lost and confused.

Knowing that their relationship was a bit much, I focused more on that as an issue and researched "mama's boy" and any variation thereof. I found out there is actually a psychological term for family members that are too close to each other. It is called *enmeshment*. Further down the road, I realized that because of this enmeshed relationship with his narcissistic mother, my husband may have become the quiet and shy version of her. Instead of being demanding and verbally abusive like her, the result may have been him becoming submissive and afraid of challenges or changes of any kind. This version of narcissism is known as *covert narcissism*.

When combining the two issues—being too close to mom and the introverted son of a narcissistic mother—I could clearly see that I had found exactly what I was looking for. I found answers and explanations for just about any question I had about my marriage, its challenges, my husband and his issues, as well as the answer to why I felt so confused and lost in the whole situation. Interestingly enough, I couldn't find any specific research on this combination, so I gave it a name: *Mother-Enmeshed Covert Narcissism*. Realizing that I was not the only one dealing with this, I decided to write a book about it to raise awareness of this issue and to provide as much information as I could. I wanted people to become aware of what I wished I had known sooner.

Let me note that due to my personal situation, I will often refer to the person exercising undue control as "the mother," the person who is enmeshed as "the husband," and the partner dealing with this mother-enmeshed person as "the wife," but rest assured, parent enmeshment and covert narcissism occur in any gender and relationship combination. Chances are you know someone whose story has similarities to mine.

I also want my readers to know that this book is not to shame my late husband or my marriage. This is about raising awareness about two different types of silent emotional abuse that can linger in any relationship. Truly, I wish I could write it without mentioning us, but I want others to learn from our situation. Not to mention that as my own intimate experience, it's the situation about which I can speak most knowledgeably.

While in real life, we went through all our trials and tribulations first and then I found explanations when our marriage had already fallen apart, I will present my book in chapters that deliver the results of my research matched with certain events as they happened. The main focus is to learn to recognize hidden red flags in a relationship with an enmeshed partner. They show up throughout the timeline and not necessarily in any particular order. But I am not here to tell my story in a perfect chronological setup. My goal is to educate, not to entertain.

You will find summaries of my research with sample anecdotes from our marriage, suggestions for dealing with different situations, and even an excerpt of my personal journal during a very traumatic time in our marriage. There will also be a section at the end of the book where readers will find suggestions on how to find peace through forgiveness, which for me was an essential step toward healing.

What I want this book to be for you as the reader is to be an eye-opener. Usually, people don't wake up one morning thinking, *Oh, there is something really wrong with us. Let's go talk to a therapist.* Most times, there is some event or gut feeling that initiates the thought of something being wrong. Then that person may start to look for clues or other people who feel the same way. In a relationship like this, it all seems surreal, and it is difficult to find the right words when talking to people without these experiences.

This is where my book comes into play. I wrote it for those who realize something is wrong but first need some sort of confirmation that they are not alone. I want my book to be *that* eye-opener, to trigger the need to find out more, google, research, read books, talk to friends, and eventually talk to a person with knowledge or even a specialist or therapist.

I want my book to be the link between having doubts and deciding to seek help or make changes.

Oh, and if you are looking for a legit research book filled with facts and stats about enmeshment and narcissism, this is not that book. I am a Google-smart everyday kind of person here to tell my story. I am not a professional or a therapist and would never claim to have the knowledge of an expert.

If you find yourself in emotional distress, I encourage you to seek support from a professional that specializes in personality disorders and who recognizes covert narcissism, as not all therapists are trained in this unique type of emotional disorder.

All in all, I hope this book will shed light in the darkness, give you hope, lift you up, and guide you to forgive those who have hurt you. I hope it gives you the ambition and desire for a new beginning! You deserve to be happy!

And know that you will be okay!

With much love from my heart to yours,
Michaela Bressel

"Getting over a painful experience is much like crossing monkey bars. You have to let go at some point in order to move forward."

—C. S. LEWIS

If you or someone you know is being mentally and/or emotionally abused, the National Domestic Violence Hotline offers 24-7 confidential and anonymous help by phone, text, or even online chat. They also assist people in finding shelters and other services.

thehotline.org / 1-800-799-SAFE (7233) / TTY 1-800-787-3224

More resources:

Love is Respect: loveisrespect.org / No More: nomore.org / Safe Horizon: safehorizon.org

---

Warning and Disclaimer:

The contents of this book are not meant to substitute for professional help and counseling. Readers are discouraged from using it for diagnostic or therapeutic purposes. The diagnosis and treatment of any personality disorder can only be done by professionals specifically trained and qualified to do so—which the author is not. The author is NOT a mental health professional.

CHAPTER 1

NARCISSISM: OVERT VERSUS COVERT

BACKGROUND STORY

NARCISSUS

Knowing very little about narcissism, I was curious to find out where the word stemmed from. I combined information from sites across the internet including Greek Mythology and Interesting Literature and came up with the following summary:

According to Greek myth, Narcissus was the son of the river god Cephissus and the nymph Liriope. He was a beautiful young hunter, and many men and women fell in love with him. However, he only showed them contempt and disdain. They often wasted away in melancholy, longing for his love because he disregarded them, while some even died from their broken hearts. Tiresias, a blind prophet, prophesied that Narcissus would grow to be an old man as long as he never looked at himself.

One day, while Narcissus was out hunting in the forest, the Oread nymph Echo spotted him and immediately fell in love with him. After Narcissus sensed someone was following him, Echo eventually revealed herself and tried to embrace him. However, he pushed her away and told her not to bother him. Echo, in the complete absence of hope, roamed around the woods for the rest of her life and wilted away until all that remained of her was the sound of an echo.

Nemesis, the goddess of retribution and revenge, found out about what had taken place and decided to penalize Narcissus for his actions. She led him to a pool; when Narcissus stopped by the water to quench his thirst, he saw his reflection in the water and fell in love with it. Wanting to kiss the beautiful vision in front of him he leaned in, not understanding it was just a reflection. When he realized his love could not materialize, he fell forward in despair and drowned.

NARCISSISTIC TRAITS
Based on the mythology of Narcissus, we often label people with a big ego or high level of self-esteem as narcissists. A solid sense of self-worth is actually something we can define as a rather positive personality trait. Mixed with other significant traits, it gives many of us the personalities we have. The quality of having an ego gives us a strong sense of self-worth, drive, and determination.

Developing an ego is a natural part of the developmental process. We literally need to love ourselves a certain amount to give us backbone, courage, self-esteem and to allow us to be happy about ourselves and the rest of the world. This healthy level of narcissism allows us to still be adaptive, flexible, and empathetic.

It needs to be added that anyone with narcissistic traits such as lacking empathy, acting obnoxious, feeling superior to others, and entitled to things, overly proud of themselves for an achievement, or having a habit of showing off is not necessarily a narcissist. While these are not personality traits that promise to allow one to make a lot of friends, they are simply traits and do not define the overall personality of the person.

Even people who like success and power and those who have feelings of being significantly above average and adored are not necessarily narcissists. This may just mean they're quite happy with themselves. And to a certain level, the worst characteristics we might ascribe to them would be selfishness, aggressiveness, egotism, or insensitivity. It is still normal to interact with someone that has elevated levels of "healthy narcissism" that end up hurting our feelings, pushing our buttons, making us mad, or leaving us feeling angry. For someone to be labeled a narcissist, they must generally have significant levels of these traits and match certain criteria, which we will discuss later in this chapter.

NARCISSISTS AS SEEN IN MOVIES
One place, albeit an imperfect one, where we can find prime examples of narcissists is in media. Many movies have been created that tell the stories of narcissistic characters. *American Psycho, Basic Instinct, Cruel Intentions, Death Becomes Her, Fatal Affair, The Hand That Rocks the Cradle, I Can Make*

You Love Me, Pretty Persuasion, Sleeping with the Enemy, and *To Die For* are just a few of them.

One movie that stuck out to me with its rampant signs of narcissism is *The Wife.* I highly recommend watching it as it is filled with the red flags my book intends to point out.

The Wife (2017, directed by Björn Runge)

This movie tells the desolate narrative of Joan Castleman (played by Glenn Close) and her husband, Joe Castleman (played by Jonathan Price) who wins the 1992 Nobel Prize for Literature. After many years of dealing with emotional abuse, Joan questions her life choices as she travels to Stockholm to see her husband receive the award.

"I hope that you know that his [love] affairs have nothing to do with you; it's a compulsion. I believe it's a deep-seated fear of inadequacy," says Nathanial Bone (played by Christian Slater) to Joan in one of the scenes about halfway through the movie. I find the quotation "deep-seated fear" to be an unintentionally perfect definition of narcissism as it is portrayed in this story.

The Castlemans' relationship started as an affair with Joan during Joe's first marriage. Their subsequent marriage then morphed into a thirty-year-long battle between the two, with Joe as the boastful and pretentious author and Joan as the submissive wife who stands by him for decades. The story reveals that Joan was actually the ghostwriter throughout his entire career. He took all the credit, as she was led to believe that a female author in the 1960s would never receive any credit for her work.

In one scene, their son David is present during one of their arguments. He cries to his father, "You made a slave of my mom," to which she interjects, "Your father doesn't control me." This reaction shows her denial of the fact that her husband has manipulated her into being submissive.

In his speech at the presentation of the Nobel Prize, Joe shows no remorse as he says to the crowd, "Really, this honor should go to someone else. My wife, Joan. Joan truly is my better half. She's made it possible for me to find the stillness, as well as the noise, to create my body of work. Without her [...] I'd be at home, staring at a blank piece of paper." Ironic how he actually tells the truth, but of course, the world has been led to believe he is the master writer. Then he goes on to invite her up to the stage. She stands up and not only leaves the gala event but also declares to him later on in private that she cannot take it any longer. "I'm leaving you," she says, to which he responds, "Don't be crazy. You're not leaving me. Don't act surprised or heartbroken or shocked, none of which you could possibly be." This reaction is clearly showing narcissistic traits like entitlement and lack of empathy.

In the next scene back at the hotel, she opens up and says that for all of those years, she was the writer sitting at the desk eight hours a day and he was the editor. His response is "Is that the way you see it? Really? What, all these years you have been sitting in some giant stew of resentment? And what about all the years I've been rubbing your back, bringing you tea, cooking your dinner, watching the kids so you could work without distraction? You don't think there were times when it killed me that you were the one with the golden touch? Hm? You think I wake up in the morning feeling even remotely proud of myself?" She goes on to pour her heart out to him how awful he has been to her for all these years. She has finally reached her breaking point.

I believe this was the most obviously narcissistic and relatable scene in the movie, as it becomes clear how Joe pushes the blame onto Joan and tries to make himself the victim while at the same time blaming her for not recognizing how much he did for her. He's careful to add in that she has the "golden touch" in an attempt to make her feel better, followed by how he's not proud of himself, yet followed by ridicule and scorn. Overall, this scene shows quite a few typical traits of narcissism within just a few minutes. I highly recommend this movie, as it served as a tool to measure my ability to recognize unhealthy behavior.

MY RESEARCH

NARCISSISTIC PERSONALITY DISORDER

Much is to be found on this disorder as narcissism has been researched for a long time. As per Britannica, "Narcissism, pathological self-absorption, [was] first identified as a mental disorder by the British essayist and physician Havelock Ellis in 1998." I found that most of the research for NPD is focused on the classic, grandiose—also known as overt—version of narcissism, which is the type that most people think of when they describe a person as being "narcissistic."

As per the Diagnostic and Statistical Manual of Mental Disorders (DSM-5), only 0.5–5 percent of the general population is diagnosed with the clinical level of *Narcissistic Personality Disorder, NPD.* To be clinically diagnosed with NPD, the person must indicate the presence of at least five of the following nine criteria:

- *A grandiose sense of self-importance (i.e., the individual exaggerates achievements and talents and expects to be recognized as superior without commensurate achievements)*
- *A preoccupation with fantasies of unlimited success, power, brilliance, beauty, or ideal love*
- *A belief that he or she is special and unique and can only be understood by, or should associate with, other special or high-status people or institutions*
- *A need for excessive admiration*
- *A sense of entitlement (i.e., unreasonable expectations of especially favorable treatment or automatic compliance with his or her expectations)*
- *Interpersonally exploitive behavior (i.e., the individual takes advantage of others to achieve his or her own ends)*
- *A lack of empathy (unwillingness to recognize or identify with the feelings and needs of others)*
- *Envy of others or a belief that others are envious of him or her*
- *A demonstration of arrogant and haughty behaviors or attitudes*

And according to a Mayo Clinic web page about NPD:

Narcissistic personality disorder—one of several types of personality disorders—is a mental condition in which people have an inflated sense of their own importance, a deep need for excessive attention and admiration, troubled relationships, and a lack of empathy for others. But behind this mask of extreme confidence lies a fragile self-esteem that's vulnerable to the slightest criticism.

A narcissistic personality disorder causes problems in many areas of life, such as relationships, work, school, and financial affairs. People with narcissistic personality disorder may be generally unhappy and disappointed when they're not given the special favors or admiration they believe they deserve. They may find their relationships unfulfilling, and others may not enjoy being around them.

Narcissistic personality disorder affects more males than females, and it often begins in the teens or early adulthood. Keep in mind that although some children may show traits of narcissism, this may simply be typical of their age and doesn't mean they'll go on to develop narcissistic personality disorder.

Although the cause of narcissistic personality disorder isn't known, some researchers think that in biologically vulnerable children, parenting styles that are overprotective or neglectful may have an impact. Genetics and neurobiology also may play a role in development of narcissistic personality disorder.

OVERT VERSUS COVERT NARCISSISM
I found it very hard to find information on covert narcissism, as it is a seemingly new term among psychologists. The

concept of covert narcissism (also termed *hypersensitivity* or *vulnerable narcissism*) was really brought into the picture by Paul M. Wink's book *Two Faces of Narcissism* in the early 90s. Wink distinguishes between overt and covert like this:

Overt: Grandiosity—Exhibitionism—related to extraversion, self-assurance, exhibitionism, and aggression

Covert: Vulnerability—Sensitivity—associated with introversion, defensiveness, anxiety, and vulnerability to life's traumas

The Verywell Mind Website states:

"Covert narcissists are only different from overt (more obvious) narcissists in that they tend to be more introverted. The overt narcissist is easily identified because they tend to be loud, arrogant, and insensitive to the needs of others and always thirsty for compliments. Their behaviors can be easily observed by others and tend to show up as 'loud and very noticeable' in a room. When we think of an overt narcissist, we could say they demonstrate mostly extroverted behaviors in their interactions with others."

It seems to me that many people have fallen victim to the manipulative behaviors of covert narcissists without realizing what was happening, as it is a lot easier to spot the extroverted (overt) narcissist than the introverted (covert) narcissist.

HIDDEN RED FLAGS IN A RELATIONSHIP WITH A COVERT NARCISSIST

In the process of my own attempt to understand all of this, I listened to an audiobook called *The Covert Passive Aggressive Narcissist: Recognizing the Traits and Finding Healing after Hidden Emotional and Psychological Abuse* by Debbie Mirza. A friend of mine suggested it to me as she too woke up from her fuzzy dream of an almost perfect relationship right into her own nightmare of the sudden, one-sided, and painful end of her ten-year marriage. My friend, an empath like me, was hurting while her partner walked away coldly and without looking back. She told me, "Micha, you need to read this book, *now*. Right now!"

And she was right. It was information that gave me assurance that I wasn't alone, I did not make this all up, and I was not at fault. It's so relieving to find a kindred soul! We share a feeling that no one else will ever understand unless they go through a similar experience. Reading this book written by Mirza really helped me see the hidden red flags in a relationship with a covert narcissist. These red flags do not *all* have to apply. This is not what defines a covert narcissist. Debbie definitely broadens the possibilities that these red flags could appear. To learn more about Debbie's work, visit debbiemirza.com, and you can also find more of her work like "20 COVERT NARCISSIST RED FLAGS" by visiting this other great site of wonderful tools and information: https://narcissistabusesupport.com.

TAKEAWAY

People suffering from NPD often experience a secret lack of self-esteem. They are fragile and insecure, commonly pushing blame on others, and often declaring themselves the victim of other people's behaviors or certain situations. They will use other people, lie, or at least withhold or distort the truth into a shape that will fit their stories and their need to achieve what benefits them. To overcome challenges, they will always seek an easy way out, often by paying money or hiring personnel to help solve an issue. Their level of self-esteem can be affected by certain events and fluctuate from high to low within moments.

Although people with NPD often describe themselves in positive terms, their subconscious feelings are often quite negative. Their daily outlook on things could be categorized like that of a "Negative Nancy," meaning there always seems to be something wrong with everything and nothing is ever good enough. Following this negativity is the constant expression of conspiracy. In their opinion, someone is always out to hurt them, especially when it comes to their financial matters.

When summarizing the information I discovered, it seems there is one very specific trait that sets apart a person with narcissistic traits from those that are actually narcissists, and that is manipulation.

It is when a narcissistic person is manipulative and takes advantage of other people regardless of the consequences that we are now looking at an abusive form of narcissism that no longer describes a simple personality trait. They are now considered a classic narcissist that doesn't show any regard for other people's feelings.

Maybe the following list will help you identify a person with narcissistic traits. The more that apply, the greater the chance you are rightfully concerned:

Does that person...

☑ ...have fantasies of unlimited power with a focus on grandiosity and elevated self-worth?

☑ ...tend to compare themselves or seek association with other "special" people? Narcissists see themselves as having a higher value than others and tend to prefer their company.

☑ ...demonstrate a sense of entitlement as if they believe the world owes them something due to an elevated view of themselves? Do they lack the ability to be humble or thankful?

☑ ...lack empathy? While being able to model empathy, their nature will usually not allow them to have this emotion.

☑ ...behave arrogantly or patronizingly? Again, based on their focus on grandiosity, they consider themselves as better beings than others.

☑ ...appear charming at every first encounter? To portray perfection and gain access to people's emotions, they often initially appear quite friendly and nice.

☑ ...chronically lie? To prevent confrontation or cover up any imperfections, they will lie. They often place themselves into an alternate reality to a point where lies become almost natural.

☑ ...give you a feeling that something is off? The victim often notices things being off but often puts the blame on themselves, engendering feelings of being lost and confused.

☑ ...tell you about all the crazy people in their past? This is often simply a deflection when they were actually at fault and the reason the situation went wrong.

Coming to the realization that someone you know might be a narcissist allows explanations not only about their behavior but also helps to explain any controversial thoughts you've had like: *It can't be narcissism because that person is so quiet and actually a very nice person.*

MOVING FORWARD

Personally, I recognized many of these symptoms in my mother-in-law as well as my husband. She represented the more grandiose version, while he was more of a vulnerable narcissist. Neither of them hesitated to use other people to achieve what was best for their own interests regardless of the cost. While she would become rather verbal in her expressions, he would instead play the victim to get attention from his listeners. They were both also quite manipulative.

Still, more research was necessary for me to fully find the answers to all my questions. Why was his relationship with his mother a constant battle when on the surface it appeared to be an impressive display of selfless love (but would later exemplify a family dynamic that lacked important boundaries)? Why did he constantly feel the need to please his mother regardless of whether that meant hurting me with lies and betrayal?

I continued searching for more information on the term "mama's boy" online, and finally, there it was. I came across a doctor that had the answer. It was explained very clearly how covert narcissism fit together with my husband's excessively close relationship with his mom. He called it MEM: *Mother Enmeshed Men.*

I had found the key that fit the lock of my dysfunctional marriage.

CHAPTER 2

MOTHER ENMESHMENT

——

BACKGROUND STORY

A TRAGEDY IN HIS EARLY YEARS

Lester's father passed away suddenly from a heart attack when Lester was only nine years of age. He told me how his mom took it very hard. She went into a deep depression, took medication, and was in the care of a psychologist for over a year. Her biggest grievance was that God had taken her husband away and that she felt left all alone to take care of her son.

On our first date, Lester told me, "One time at a family gathering, sometime after my dad died, someone said to my mom, 'Kathy, you need to go out there and find a new husband!' I jumped up and said, 'My mom doesn't need a husband, she has me to take care of her.' And so, I did. She never remarried, and I am keeping my promise to take care of her for the rest of her life."

He also told me how she would remind him of that promise over the years, essentially placing the marital responsibilities of a husband onto Lester. While it may not seem like much, for a son, that can be overwhelming, as he should not have had to burden himself with that responsibility. As a result, Lester did not really have a chance to grieve the loss of his father. Instead, the attention was now on his mother's pain and suffering, which Lester, now being responsible for his mother, took quite to heart. Losing a spouse is devastating, yes. But losing a parent at the age of nine can also be very traumatic. Almost anyone would expect that a mother would put her own feelings aside to protect and comfort her child. In this case though, Kathy drew the attention away from Lester's loss of a father and redirected it toward the loss of her husband.

The more I researched, the more I realized that these two events—the mother's breakdown paired with Lester's promise to take care of his mother—may have been the root of Lester's emotional immaturity. Lester had learned that his mother's emotions and feelings took priority over his, and Kathy had begun to raise him in the belief that it was his responsibility to take care of her in place of her husband. The way he loved his mother at the time was appropriate to that of a nine-year-old. At that age, he listened to what his mother said and tried to make her happy regardless of his own mind on the matter. But at this age, children should also be given the opportunity to explore boundaries and discover their own needs and wants. It is easy to see that laying the responsibility to take care of his mother on Lester could have ruined this opportunity for him. It laid down the path to not fully developing his self-worth, leading him to have low self-esteem and other emotional issues later.

―――――――――

Conducted with the aim of developing the Childhood Emotional Incest Scale (CEIS), the present study supports the idea that emotional incest may force children to sacrifice their childhood in an attempt to satisfy the emotional needs of lonely and/or needy parents and that it leads to decreased life satisfaction and increased anxiety in adult children.

—JOURNAL OF COUNSELING PSYCHOLOGY

―――――――――

MORE THAN A MAMA'S BOY

In summary, I think Lester was a very disconsolate child, as he was disliked not only by his peers, but he also didn't like himself while his mother seemed more concerned with how his education would reflect on her. The emotional stress of taking on his father's role at a young age took a toll on Lester's overall health, physically and mentally. Lester struggled with a lack of self-confidence and a high level of anxiety for the remainder of his life.

While his mother was struggling financially after his father's death, she placed Lester into an upscale Catholic school in one of the suburbs of Los Angeles. "I was the poor kid in a rich school," Lester relayed in one of our conversations. She neglected to see the negative effect this had on Lester. The kids in school knew what neighborhood he lived in and often teased or even bullied him for this reason.

On top of that, he was also always the chubby kid, which gave the other pupils even more reason to make fun of him. He mentioned that his weight issues were his grandmother's fault. According to what his mom would tell him, deflecting the blame away from her, his grandmother would give him too many sodas as a child. Throughout school, he was not directly involved in sports, band, music, or any type of extracurricular activities. It seems the focal point of his childhood was directed mostly by his mother's desire for him to reach a certain status in life through education, disregarding any interests or desires that Lester may have had.

When I was looking through his report cards, there was one from eighth grade where the teacher noted, "He seems to like himself a little better this year." Reading that broke my heart, as it showed me that he struggled with his self-image enough that a teacher would note improvement on a grade report.

In his late teenage years, Lester's lack of self-love degenerated into anxiety and depression. Instead of searching for the source of his problems, Kathy found a doctor that would medicate his problems in the same way she controlled her own depression. Adding to his depleting self-esteem were his growing struggles with his weight.

Over the years, Lester had tried many different "As Seen on TV" offers to improve his weight. From twenty-one-day cleanses and insane workout programs to hormone treatments, he had tried about any shortcut and diet pill to lose the extra pounds. Despite these attempts, he never fully accomplished managing his weight. He started on many different regimens but didn't finish any of them. While he stuck to testosterone shots the longest, the workout DVDs were still in their wrappers when I found them. He didn't seem to worry about the visual side—the effects of hormones on him like man boobs, acne, excessive body hair, and balding—as much as he disliked the actual effort and consistency other programs would require to get results.

As for my husband's feelings toward his mother? Well, I would describe it as a love-hate relationship. I know he felt love for her. He somewhat even worshiped her like a child worships a parent when they are little. He never really expressed his love to her directly other than the "I love yous" that were at the end of their phone conversations. He would defend her actions or bad behavior toward me but also have outbursts of how helpless he felt to not be able to voice his opinion. He also told me about the resentment he felt about her hitting him when he was younger.

He told stories about how she had embarrassed him in front of his friends to the point that he hardly had any kids come over. Furthermore, he knew that she lied to him and kept secrets from him. He complained that she didn't tell him where his income went. He told me that she managed it all, and he felt like he was just there to earn it. While he had no idea where it all went, he still always told her first, asked her first, consulted with her first before making decisions about his own spending.

RESPONSIBLE FOR MOM

On many occasions, it came up that his mother was the one making all the decisions regarding his finances. It was quite clear that Kathy was spending more money than what Lester brought home in earnings. And this started way back when he was still in college. Those days, she may have worked a few jobs like ironing or cleaning people's homes. But with him being in school plus the added expenses for higher education, there wasn't enough money to support her growing desire for an elevated lifestyle.

"But why wouldn't you say anything? You were not responsible for her!" I'd ask him.

"What choice did I have? I had to quit college so I could find a job instead," was his answer.

He seemed quite angry with his mom when we talked about how she was in control. At the same time, he seemed frustrated and ashamed, as it showed how little power he had over his mother. For all those years, he had no idea where all of the money that he brought home went. She kept buying things either to pretty up the house or update features that were unnecessary.

"Why don't you just tell her that from here on out you'll decide what happens with the money?" I would ask.

His face would lose its strong expression, and he would respond with something like, "I tried, but there is nothing I can do about it. I don't really have a say in that."

There was the house in LA where they lived before they moved to Las Vegas. She spent a lot of money to renovate it from top to bottom with a new kitchen, bathrooms, and yard landscaping. It was sold with a huge profit, but instead of being smart about it and using it toward equity of the new home in Las Vegas, she spent it all on lavish upgrades like tile floors, marble counters, and a fully landscaped backyard with a pool and Jacuzzi. It was only a year later that they filed bankruptcy and refinanced the home as the debt kept growing on small loans and countless credit cards.

It never seemed to have mattered how Lester felt. It only mattered what his mom expected regardless of the cost. His decisions were based on her desires, happiness, and satisfaction. He disregarded what made sense or what would have been considered smart budgeting.

LESTER'S WARDROBE—UNVARIED AND MOTHER APPROVED

The first time I got a peek into Lester's closet was a few weeks after we met. The first thing I noticed was its perfect appearance. His clothes were color-coordinated, hanging from light to dark, consisting of four or five of the same shirt or shorts, mostly from the same brand. As for his bottoms, they were all basketball-style shorts made of a polyester mesh and either white or black. His socks were crew cut, also white or black, neatly folded in half, and stacked in sets of three in the dresser. All his clothes, including the socks and undergarments, looked ironed, and none had holes or stains.

When I pointed out how immaculate everything looked, he blushed a little and told me that it was all his mom's doing.

"She takes care of all that. She puts them up after the wash, lays them out for the next day, and replaces them when needed. It makes it simple. I don't have to worry about it or wonder what to wear the next day, and it makes her happy," he said. He had a few other shirts, mostly themed with audio installation designs or souvenir-type shirts. He'd gotten those himself, he said.

He had two pairs of leather athletic shoes he'd wear: a white pair and a black pair—both the same brand and same style. As soon as he took off a pair, she would clean them, polish the top, and wipe the bottom. In the mornings, when he was getting ready to go to work, she made sure to put them in front of him when he was sitting in the living room recliner. There was always a brand-new pair of each in the closet in case she felt the need to replace the not-so-old looking old pair.

What didn't seem so apparent at first became so very obvious over time. Most days, he wore all white on white or all black on black, from shirt to shorts to socks and shoes. At first, I thought it was color coordination simplified or maybe a hint of OCD. Later, I got the feeling it was more a lack of having a personal preference. While he claimed this *was* his preference, I think he adapted to what his mom kept buying for him. Sticking to the same type of clothes ensured that everything from the ease of cleaning to the matching and replacement remained simple and conflict free between Kathy and Lester.

BATHROOM HABITS—LIKE MOTHER LIKE SON

Like many people, I have daily routines. I do things in a certain order. Most people I know do the same, but Lester's morning and evening bathroom routines were literally identical every day. It was like experiencing déjà vu watching him.

And on top of that, some of his habits were just plain uncommon. I want to give you a heads up. There will be personal details that may be uncomfortable to read. But also, please keep in mind that I am not here to shame my husband but to point out hidden red flags and signs of mother enmeshment.

Brushing his teeth in the mornings, with both arms leaning on the sink and toothpaste drooling out of his mouth, he would initiate his gag reflexes for a few moments. He'd then let the foam-filled brush fall in the sink while he flushed his mouth with water, rinsed, dried the brush, and put it back into the neatly organized top drawer between the double sinks. It wasn't the fact that he kept a routine that I found to be off, it was the realization that they were exactly the same moves each and every time.

When we lived together, about an hour before bedtime, he'd fill the bathtub to the rim—no soap. He told me that before me, things were a bit different. His mom would fill the tub for him just in time for when he came home from work. Kathy would lay out a fresh towel and line up his shaving utilities. She would bring him little snacks while he was sitting in the tub. Maybe some cut up apples or sometimes a cup of coffee, but she always brought him something.

Usually, he would brush his teeth while in the water, using the tub water to rinse and spit, followed by a shave if needed.

Again, it wasn't that it was a routine that was strange, it was the fact that his mom assisted him with it until I came along. I also knew when he went to his mom's after work instead of coming home, she would have the tub water ready for him like in the old days. It bothered me that he would take a bath there even though we lived in our own home. They kept up certain routines in "their home" even though he had moved out. To me, it felt like he was hesitant to fully commit to me while assuring his mom that he had not completely left her care.

Then there was something that seemed very personal and even awkward for me to think about —even more awkward to write it into words. It was the way he urinated. I know. You may think I am crazy to write about that. But it is all part of the big picture, piece by piece. Not only would he sit down to pee, but he also would face the water tank. It was always awkward to me. Having raised kids, this reminded me of a small boy learning how to use the bathroom. I can just imagine that this is how his mom taught him to pee when he was little, and he had never developed his own preference, as this was how his mom had showed him. Forgive me if I am out of line and don't realize that maybe other men use the bathroom like this. I never asked him, as I didn't want him to be embarrassed, but to me it looked backward and childlike.

Kathy would also take a bath every night, and while she had her own bathroom, she never used it for taking her baths. She used his bathroom for her baths. And mind you, there was no door between the master bedroom and the attached master bath. It grossed me out to think there must have been times when dressing or undressing occurred with the other one present. And he admitted to me that this was nothing unusual. He said he didn't feel bothered that she was freely walking in on him at any time he was not wearing clothes.

Over time, it became more and more clear that it was Kathy keeping up the motherly involvement in his life, while Lester seemed not to know anything different and to never think to demand changes in her behavior. What Kathy and Lester failed to apply were healthy boundaries.

MY RESEARCH

DESPERATE FOR ANSWERS

Many hours of googling and searching for keywords like "when a son loves his mother more than a wife" or "sons too close to their mothers" went by until I stumbled across a very important and eye-opening website for a book called *When He's Married to Mom: How to Help Mother-Enmeshed Men Open Their Hearts to True Love and Commitment* by Dr. Kenneth Adams, a licensed psychologist and internationally recognized expert in treating trauma-induced intimacy disorders. A part of the website article reads as follows:

"One in ten men in America has excessive emotional ties to their mothers. Referred to as mother-son enmeshment, this potentially damaging relationship occurs when sons serve as surrogate husbands for their lonely and neglected mothers

who rely on their sons for closeness and emotional support.
It can create major issues for these mother-enmeshed men
(MEMS)—commitment phobia, guilt, feelings of inadequacy,
and low self-worth, to name just a few—which, in turn, can
lead to ambivalence and indecision in adult relationships."

My stomach went into a knot when I read this. Every word
in this description fit Lester's situation—every single word.

And another excerpt from the same book confirmed my sus-
picion that I may have found the answer I was looking for:

> *"In his unconscious—and sometimes conscious—mind, a*
> *mother-enmeshed man is representing his mother's inter-*
> *ests, while his own have become secondary. If he does*
> *something he thinks she wouldn't like, he feels disloyal to*
> *her. If he 'gets serious' about a woman, suddenly, with-*
> *out understanding why, he is overwhelmed with feelings*
> *of fear, anxiety, and guilt. Ambivalence and withdrawal*
> *inevitably follow."*

Now that I had a specific topic to look for, *mother enmeshment*, I realized that not only were there not very many articles and books about enmeshment in general but there were
even fewer specifically about a mother and her son. I did
come across another helpful article by emotion and relational
therapist trainee Rachel Anyika that confirmed that Lester's
lack of emotional maturity could very well have originated
from his childhood:

"Enmeshment (also known as emotional incest) happens when
a child is required to take on an adult role in their relationship

with a parent (or caregiver). *This often occurs where one parent is physically or emotionally absent, which causes the other parent to use the child as an emotional crutch or substitute for an adult relationship. It can also occur when one parent has a serious illness or physical disabilities and cannot fully look after themselves without assistance from the child. In both instances, the parents' needs have taken over the child's individual emotional needs. The most common form of enmeshment which causes wide ranging effects on relationships, is that of mother enmeshed men, as a result of an emotionally underdeveloped, needy mother and an absent or emotionally absent father. Much of the blueprint we have for (heterosexual) relationships comes from the relationship we had with the opposite sex parent. Therefore, enmeshed men are carrying forward enmeshment trauma into their adult relationships.*"

PETER PAN SYNDROME

Further into my research, I came across a book called *Narcissist and the Peter Pan Syndrome*. The subtitle of this book, *Emotionally Unavailable and Emotionally Immature Men*, was also what caught my attention. Just by glancing over the description on Amazon, I saw characteristics that paralleled Lester's personality as a child and an adult:

Many people have heard about the Peter Pan syndrome. The term was coined by Dr. Dan Kiley in the book The Peter Pan Syndrome: Men Who Have Never Grown Up. [...] We have all met men who have the Peter Pan syndrome. Many of these men are also narcissistic and self-absorbed simply by the nature of the Peter Pan syndrome. A man who is stuck in his path through life as a boy never matures emotionally. He carries around his childhood sense of himself throughout his life. In many instances, his tastes do not grow or change. The way that he interacts with others does not grow or change. He is still stuck as a 12-year-old boy, or sometimes even younger, in his emotional development."

Reading just that bit of information reminded me so much of Lester. He did seem "stuck" in his feelings and emotions. And I believe for Lester, it all started when his father passed away. It was *that* moment that changed everything, the moment he stopped growing into an adult, the moment that his mother became the focal point in his life—or better yet, the moment his mother made herself the focal point in his life, the moment when it no longer mattered what he felt, needed, or wanted, the moment when the only thing that mattered was his mother.

TAKEAWAY

From what I was learning, I realized that this enmeshment would have effects on the grown man's personal well-being, his behavior toward others like friends or coworkers, and especially any romantic relationship he may try to enter.

The effects mainly manifest in these areas:

- Self-Confidence
- Emotional Intimacy
- Personality

Let's take a closer look at these individual subjects.

SELF-CONFIDENCE

No matter if this is early on or later in life, the mother-enmeshed man (MEM) will more than likely lack self-confidence. This is very easily explained upon realizing that the MEM has always been valued by his mother for what he's done and not for who he is. His efforts to impress another person—and especially a woman—will always be based on what he does for others. He will appear to be generous by lending money to friends and leaving large tips for the waitress or service personnel. He will love bomb a woman that he courts to impress her by buying expensive gifts, taking her for nice dinners, vacations, and of course buying an impressive home. He will do anything that he believes will show the woman he is trying to impress that he has value. This will give him a false sense of confidence and will not allow him to realize that he lacks it. Thus, when asking a MEM if he lacks confidence, he will assure you this is not the case, while deep inside, he will always battle anxiety, having trouble believing in his self-worth.

INTIMACY

The MEM will experience difficulties engaging in intimate relationships. Finding someone will not be hard for him, as he knows how to emotionally fulfill a woman's needs. Even physically, he will not hesitate to satisfy the woman. But to deeply commit will be nearly impossible, as his loyalty is already given to his mother and his understanding of love usually ends up with feeling angry or guilty. He will not seek individuality; he will do what he believes will make the woman happy, disregarding how he may feel about it. On the other hand, the MEM will try to separate from the mother at first, but the feeling of betrayal will take over, causing an emotional conflict within him, keeping him from truly letting another woman into his life. Any relationship will lack deep emotional intimacy, as his loyalty will always go to the mother.

PERSONALITY

With the underdevelopment of his own needs, wants, and desires comes a lack of true personality. The MEM will embody the person that he believes another person would expect from him. He will play his role well, but it will not reflect his own imagination. He will lack true hobbies, likes, or dislikes, as he is programmed to accommodate the person he is with. When offered choices, his decisions will be based on what he believes is expected from him. He will absorb knowledge quickly but will lack imagination. When confronted with options, choices, or challenges, he will choose the path of least resistance, as he does not handle decision-making very well. Using his common sense or his own ideas when planning ahead will be rare, while basing decisions based on previous events will be done without effort. This also explains why the MEM is a creature of habit and why changes are not something the MEM handles easily.

HOW TO IDENTIFY ENMESHMENT?

The first step is to determine if there is in fact an enmeshment present or if it is a close but healthy relationship between a mother and her son. Keep in mind that there is no exact definition. Lester and his mom's relationship inspired me to put these symptoms together:

- [x] Do they share an intense collaboration on daily routines and activities?

- [x] Do they have the same or similar level of interest in a diversity of areas?

- [x] Does the mother seem to inflict her interests onto her son?

- [x] Does the son lack individuality—meaning his own hobbies and interests?

- [x] Does it seem the son agrees to everything just to please the mother?

- [x] Does the mother seem to live vicariously through her son's activities?

- [x] Do they seem often to have similar expectations from each other for how to feel or respond to situations?

- [x] Is the son unable to express his feelings toward his mother without either feeling extreme anxiety or depression?

- [x] Are there clear boundaries separating the two individuals, or does everything seem to be a "we, us, and ours?"

- [x] Are there boundaries set in matters of privacy (especially in the bathroom and bedroom)?

- [x] Does he seem to feel the way she does—when she is happy, he is happy, and when she is sad, he is sad, etc.?

☑ Does he seem to change his opinion if he feels the mother doesn't agree with him?

The above listed symptoms often start when the child is little and last long into adulthood, and the more that apply, the bigger the chance the relationship is of an unhealthy nature.

MOVING FORWARD

Having learned all about the indicators that my husband was a victim of parent enmeshment by reflecting on his child-hood, I saw a direct connection to the issues in our marriage and the broken relationship between my mother-in-law and me. The more I learned about enmeshment, the easier it became to see the hidden red flags in my relationship with Lester. The lies and distortion of truth as well his longing for money and wealth to solve all his issues became more and more clear to be a product of Kathy's close involvement in Lester's daily affairs.

But that was after I did my research, after my marriage was broken, and after I already felt hurt, lost, and confused.

Before all of that, my world was perfect!

From waking up into total darkness to going down memory lane and meeting the "cute couple" –you will find it in the next chapter!

CHAPTER 3

SOULMATES

BACKGROUND STORY

WAKING UP TO TOTAL DARKNESS

Mother-enmeshed men. Covert narcissism. Silent emotional abuse. How come I had never even heard of these issues until my world was falling apart? It took me eight years of living through them, blinded by the beautiful love I thought myself to be surrounded by.

How can they call it unhealthy if a mother loves her son more than usual? How can it be narcissism if there is no hurtful bullying or excessive outbursts of anger? And how can it be abuse if there is no violence? And yet, these are the words often used when reading about a relationship with a mother-enmeshed covert narcissist.

It seems so surreal. I catch myself wanting to call him and talk to him like in the old days, but he is gone.

We were so very happy together. Our marriage seemed indestructible even with everything that we had been through. Memories of our marriage keep popping up on my social media profile, portraying a wide variety of our ups and downs. It reminds me of the fun times we had: on our date nights, going out to a bar or playing pool, our honeymoon that we spent on a cruise while forgetting the world around us and feeling like kids on an adventure trip, the accident when I almost lost him and the brain injury that left him without speech for a few months, all of the lies that I forgave him for as I truly believed he only lied to protect my happiness, the pain I felt when he divorced me after the accident, the nearly two years I spent fighting to get him back until we got remarried, the almost three years that he was in prison to pay for the crimes he'd committed for and with his mom, the strength it took at first to forgive Kathy to then being by her side in the last weeks of her life, the excitement when he came home, followed by the last lie that ended it all.

At that time, many thoughts of doubt and betrayal were stirring in my mind. "Do not let him win! This is real. He never loved you. He said he did, he acted as if he did, he made you feel like he did, but it was all a pretend world. Look around, Micha! You are not with him. You are heartbroken while he's walked away and won't even talk to you. You do not exist anymore in his world. Everything you think of is forgotten and has no value to him." At that time, my mind still tried to connect the dots of all that had happened, making me think things like, *I am worthless. I failed. I caused this. I did not do enough. I should have reacted differently. I should not have blamed him or called him a liar again. I should have done better.*

The illusion of us as a perfect couple had come to an end. The endless lies had stripped me down to my shell with nothing left to fight for. I felt empty, lifeless, and weak. But I knew I did not give up on us. I gave out and walked away in September of 2020.

Little did I know, just six months later while still writing this book, I would actually lose him forever.

Now more than ever before, I want to fill this book with stories, facts, love, and suggestions to others who may also feel like they've woken up from a beautiful dream into the reality of a dreadful nightmare.

Here is where my dream began...

FEELING THE BUTTERFLIES

I made sure my makeup was subtle but flattering and that my hair was tucked nicely into a bun. I was nervously looking at the clock like it would make time go by faster as I cut ham, mixed mayonnaise with tuna, and did all the other prep work involved in making sandwiches. It wasn't the job I had come to Las Vegas to do, but I had to make a living somehow as I worked my way into establishing my position as a health coach and weight loss specialist at a local wellness club. On this sunny but cold day in early January while working on chores at work, I found myself sidetracked and absentminded. Nervously I kept looking into the customer area, trying to spot the gentleman I'd met a few days prior during an initial wellness consultation concerning weight loss. Our first encounter turned into a lively two-hour conversation about this and that and less about his desire to improve his health. We ended up exchanging phone numbers and decided to meet again but privately. He told me he was working as a security officer in one of the big casinos and was going to stop by to make sure we were still on for our first date.

The front door of the restaurant opened, and there he was, dressed all in black. He seemed nervous and had both hands in his pockets while wearing a timid smile. I could tell he was excited to stand in line—not to order a sandwich, but to ask for me.

"There's a guy asking for you," a coworker said.

"Oh?" I responded as if I didn't know what it was about. I washed my hands quickly and glanced in the mirror hanging on the wall once more to make sure I looked as polished as I could in my uniform and apron.

"Hello, Micha," he said rather shyly. "Are we still on for our date Tuesday night?"

"Yes," I replied "I can't wait! Where are we going?" I asked.

"You'll see. I'll surprise you! Pick you up at six?" he responded with excitement in his voice.

"That would be great. I'll be ready. Evening attire?"

"You'll look beautiful in anything, but yes, evening attire would be great!" he said.

The day was Sunday, January 6, 2013—the day after we'd met. Tuesday couldn't have come fast enough.

OUR FIRST DATE

I kept looking through the balcony sliding door to see if he was entering the apartment complex. At six o'clock sharp, his black BMW with tinted windows pulled around the corner. I grabbed my purse and ran down the stairs. Again, he looked a bit nervous, but he held his head high as he stepped out, walked around the car, and opened my door, as a gentleman would. The car was spotless inside and out. The paint sparkled in the lights that illuminated the parking lot, and the interior smelled freshly cleaned, accented by the aroma of a black scent tree hanging from the mirror. Our conversations consisted of random chattering while we drove to the Strip, parked at the Bellagio, and walked through the casino.

"Here we are. I made a reservation for us," he said with excitement in his voice.

I looked up and saw that we were at one of the finest steakhouses on the entire Strip. The restaurant host walked us to a little table by the wall that had a candle in the middle, as elegant as could be. I was not used to being treated so fancily, and my heart felt like it was jumping out of my chest.

This guy really knows how to make an impression, I thought to myself.

We ordered food and drinks while talking about all sorts of things. As he expressed interest in my plans for 2013, I pulled up a photo on my phone of a vision board I had created the same day we had met at the health club for his consultation. It showed goals that I had set for the new year, among them a big house, flight tickets for my kids to visit, a lady in a beautiful wedding gown, a picture of a female bodybuilder, cash in savings, my own wellness store, and a wedding band, and in the middle was a cutout from a magazine of a yellow Porsche. He seemed quite taken and impressed that I had so many goals set for the near future.

"You will accomplish all of this and more; I am sure of it," he said with confidence.

In our conversation, he told me that besides working as a security guard at one of the major casinos on the Las Vegas Strip, his main income actually came from something much bigger. With pride, he told me he was the one who did all the car audio installations for the TV series 24. It was there that he had made a name for himself, and he was working for another employer in the same industry located farther north in California. This other employer kept him coming back almost every weekend to work on high-priced car brands like Porsche, Maserati, etc. The pay apparently was outstanding and included reimbursement for his car rental and lodging expenses.

He said he'd drive thirteen hours to get there, do twelve hours of work, then drive back again. It sounded exhausting. He explained that the economy had plunged just after buying a house and moving to Las Vegas with his mother. Since then, finances were tight, but he would only do this until all the bigger bills were paid up to date. "Hopefully just a few more years," he mentioned. It all sounded impressive, especially hearing that he was supporting his mother and she was accompanying him on every single trip for the past six years he had been doing this. I couldn't think of any mother being that devoted to her adult child. Six years is a long time to endure those long drives and not once miss the opportunity to keep him company. After our fancy dinner, just when I thought nothing could top this beautiful evening, he had another surprise for me. We walked through the casino and ended up at the entrance of "O," an extravagant aquatic circus performance. Too shy to make a move, we watched the show, giggling like kids in our seats.

I really enjoyed getting to know him. He was a few years younger than I was, but nothing too significant. His hair was stylish, voluminous, and parted neatly to the side. His cologne caught my attention but wasn't overwhelming, and his manners were impeccable. He spoke very highly of his mom, which mattered to me, as I had always been told to look for a man who treats his mother with respect. And quite obviously from his stories, he seemed to worship her. *What a keeper*, I thought to myself, knowing I wanted to see him again. We started dating, and after two weeks finally broke the ice with our first kiss.

At the beginning, everything may seem perfect—maybe even too perfect. You might think you've found someone who is not only into you but also showers you with attention, love, gifts, and more—like, all of the validation and affirmation you've

been waiting for. But then, your relationship may later turn
into something you don't even recognize.

COSMOPOLITAN, "HERE'S EVERYTHING YOU NEED TO KNOW
ABOUT LOVE BOMBING AND WHY IT'S SO DANGEROUS"

THE HOUSE—A SHOWCASE OF A HOME

We dated for a couple of weeks before he invited me to come to his house. I remember when I first walked inside. Everything looked extremely neat and clean. The entire interior was painted in a very light yellow, accented with white window frames and interior shutters. There were countless decorative pieces of silver, chrome, and royal blue throughout the house, giving the impression of a showcase home. There were hardly any items for use, and even if they were, they were displayed in a decorative way. There was no particular smell or feeling. It was tasteful but tasteless at the same time. Expensive items were arranged side by side to be seen and admired. Many crystal glass items mixed with silver platters filled several curio cabinets in the dining room. The hallway had no pictures or traditional wall decor, just twelve mirror tiles glued in a diamond pattern. I considered it simply boring back then. *They must like seeing themselves*, I thought, thinking that was funny. The beds in Kathy's and Lester's rooms looked like those in a fine hotel: flawless and without a wrinkle in them.

The landscaped backyard reminded me of a Greek garden, the pool and Jacuzzi were lined with blue tiles, a few midsize concrete statues were placed along the backside of the pool, and every pebble or rock seemed strategically placed.

There was a round concrete table and a bench with surfaces made of pieces of blue tiles and glass, and the cinder block walls surrounding the property were decorated with leftover floor tiles that hung on their point in a symmetrical pattern, accented with leftover tiles from the pool. Blue was apparently his mom's favorite color to decorate the interior as well as the exterior of the house.

THE GUY OF MY DREAMS—HE'S PERFECT!

Only a month after we met, he surprised me with a romantic weekend in Malibu. He chose one of the most expensive beach hotels there. He got us a beautiful room with a balcony overlooking the waves below. Breakfast was served on a terrace also overlooking the beach. It was all quite classy, and we were treated like royalty. I was quite flattered to be treated so specially, while he seemed quite content in these exquisite surroundings. *Finally, a man that has his life together, is worry-free and works hard enough to spoil me a little*, I thought to myself. Not that I had had any expectations, but it sure felt good and made me feel appreciated. And after having gone through a few rough spots in life myself, this was such a delight!

For Valentine's Day, which, mind you, was just a month and a half after we first met, he revealed that he had a surprise for our dinner date. When the time came to pick me up, the security gate to my apartment complex opened, and there came this cute little Porsche Boxster driving around the corner. It was bright yellow in color, which reminded me of the one on my vision board, just an older model.

"I'm sorry I'm late," he said, looking up to the balcony where he had spotted me waiting. "I went to LA to pick up this car!"

"That's a cute little car. Did you trade in the BMW?" I asked curiously.

"No," he said cheerfully. "I got this for you! Happy Valentine's! Come on down and look at it!"

I flew down the stairs, holding a Valentine's card that I had made him, and fell into his arms. I started to cry. I lost my breath, as I was sobbing like a little kid when I handed him my little card.

"Happy Valentine's baby! I got you a card," I said, trying to wipe away the tears that had already halfway washed off my makeup out of gratitude for this extravagant gift. He noticed the greeting card I gave him was handmade.

"You made this?" he asked, and now his eyes filled with tears as he started crying. "No one's ever made me a card." He lowered his eyes, wrapped his arms around me, and held me tight for a few moments.

We decided we needed to dry up our tears and just enjoy the moment. After all, it was Valentine's Day, and we were going on a romantic date. He asked if I wanted to drive, but I was too nervous, so he drove. We had a nice dinner at a nearby sushi place. It was there that I expressed my respect for him for taking care of his mom for the past thirty years. I told him I was sure it took a lot to do that. Again, his eyes filled with tears.

"I appreciate you saying that. It means a lot to me. This is usually when women run away. I love my mom, and she will always be part of my life." He seemed so relieved to know I liked the fact that he cared that much about her.

DREAMS DO COME TRUE!

Just a few weeks later, Lester asked me to go house rental shopping for us. I was so thrilled to hear he wanted to move in together after such a short time. He wanted me to find us a big house to rent with a yard near the community where he lived so he could be close to his mom in case she needed anything. The home I found met all his suggestions, and the lease started on the first of March, barely three months after we'd met. It all went so fast! It was almost a bit scary, but I'd fallen in love with this man so quickly, and he seemed to love me back. Being with him felt amazing. I felt so loved for the first time in a very long time.

It wasn't the car or the weekend by the beach or the idea of living in a big rental house itself—it was the fact that this guy would do literally anything for me right off the bat. *He must be quite serious about being with me if he's putting so much effort into treating me like his queen,* I thought. It felt really good to be loved by him. I was a bit intimidated when I found out that he paid the whole year's lease amount in cash. In the past, I was happy if I was able to pay my rent for the next month on time. But it gave me assurance that Lester was serious about being together.

From then on, it seemed he was always reading my mind, surprising me with little treats that I must have mentioned at some point. For example, he must have noticed that I loved Nutella when he came home one evening with fine Nutella-filled baked goods from the patisserie at the casino. Another day I must have brought up that I really needed a haircut, so he called the beauty shop and set up an appointment as a surprise. Lester was the most caring man ever. No man had ever spoiled me like that, and I enjoyed every moment of it. As a matter of fact, I didn't want it to end— ever. I even caught myself imagining how it would be to be married to this amazing gentleman.

Admiring the fact that I was a health coach and loved going to the gym, he supported my idea of joining a figure competition. In the beginning of April of that year, he financed my way to prepare and train for the Las Vegas Classic, one of the larger body building events in our city. I had six months to prepare, and thanks to Lester's generous funding, I had one of the top trainers in town and was able to focus 100 percent on the proper foods and workout sessions.

Lester continued to spoil me. It seemed that everything I hoped to accomplish—the things that I had had on my vision board that he had seen on our first date—came true with his help, including seeing my four grown kids. In May, he bought both of us flight tickets so that we could be at one of my daughter's graduation; just a month later, he paid for my kids to fly to Las Vegas to spend time with me. Lester helped give the kids an amazing experience by funding rides, dinners, and excursions all around town. I was so happy to be able to see my children, and I knew I could not have done it without him. I really believed at that point that by creating my vision board, I had called all these things into existence simply by meeting the man of my dreams.

And his generosity didn't end there. Before the year was over, Lester provided me with the funds to open a wellness store. It was quite a costly investment, but he didn't mind and seemed rather proud to be able to help me fulfill all the goals I had set. Everything was just so perfect. He seemed excited to be the owner, even though helping was not much on his agenda. Eventually, he quit the security job in the spring of 2015. While I was at the store working with clients, he would stop by, but I knew he was spending a lot of time with his mother. Truth is, I found myself getting upset about the imbalances in his attention toward her versus me and our store. But I kept reminding myself that if it weren't for his funding, I wouldn't have had the wellness store at all. I felt that I was not in the position to complain, so I didn't.

Other than that, I was the happiest girl in the whole wide world. We enjoyed going out to the movies, dinner dates, shows, and exhibitions up and down the Las Vegas Boulevard. For nearly a year and a half, everything was so very wonderful. We never fought, we didn't seem to have any complaints about anything, and our love was one to be envied.

TYING THE KNOT

After the second year of being together, we decided to get married. It was more me than him that was ready for this next step. I couldn't wait to be his wife! Lester, however, seemed a bit hesitant and nervous. Kathy had caused quite a few disagreements between us by then and was not very happy about us tying the knot. This left Lester filled with anxiety to even mention it to his mom. He was hurt by the realization that he couldn't get his mother's approval for something he wanted to be excited and happy about.

I was convinced that once we were joined in marriage, his mom would back off, knowing there was nothing further she could do to prevent Lester from dedicating the rest of his life to us instead of only her. For our engagement, he arranged a nice dinner at the same restaurant we'd had our first date. We sat at our little table for two, chatting away happily, and by the time dessert was being served, the staff had surrounded us with candlelight. Then he got on one knee and asked the question, "Micha, will you be my wife?" I felt like I was in heaven; this was what I wished for with all my heart! He presented the ring we had carefully chosen: an assembly of three beautiful rings, the middle diamond band in white gold serving as the engagement ring and the outer two diamond bands in yellow gold, all matching the striping of the matching band for him. They were perfect! And now that it was official, Lester seemed relieved and excited to start a new chapter as husband and wife.

The wedding was just after Christmas 2015. It was a small but absolutely beautiful ceremony at the Venetian, one of the major casinos in Las Vegas. The procession was in a white wedding gondola that floated down the indoor riverways of the resort. We arranged for a picture package and dining room reception for about thirty guests. Of course, just prior to the event, his mother tried to draw attention to herself by letting Lester know she would not be attending. It was only after talking her out of her stubbornness that she agreed to join the reception. Even without her blessing, it turned out to be a very beautiful wedding and a day to remember forever.

For our honeymoon, Lester arranged a seven-day cruise to Belize for us on the world's third-largest cruise ship to leave harbor just a few days after the wedding. After reading up on tips for packing for a cruise, I was prepared to stack and squeeze everything into a tiny cabin. To my surprise, he got us the biggest suite that included a bedroom, living area, kitchenette, an oversized bathroom, and a double balcony with a breathtaking view from the tenth level of the ship. It was a perfect vacation and a much-needed getaway for us two lovebirds.

The first couple of years seemed like a dream, and I was convinced that we were made for each other. No matter what I said, he loved it, agreed, or at least supported my opinion. And I loved everything about him. He was perfect! He seemed to want to make sure everything I ever wished for came true. All I saw was that he was the ultimate example of a loving husband. It appeared he would do little for himself and everything for me. I was living the dream and had undoubtedly found my soulmate...

MY RESEARCH

While remembering these first two years as the happiest of my life, I realized much later that there were many hidden red flags of something being wrong. I did not see them because I was blinded by all the magic and the wonderful things in our relationship. This significant tactic seen in people with narcissistic traits is known as *Love Bombing*.

LOVE BOMBING—A NARCISSIST'S TOOL TO CONVINCE AND DISTRACT

Sending flowers, planning romantic getaways, being thoughtful and understanding about everything, lots of romantic conversation, detailed talks about our future, and long periods of staring into each other's eyes had me head over heels in love with Lester. From the moment we met, I was convinced that I had found my soulmate. What I didn't realize was that with all these gifts, I was so taken that I would overlook his actions that were not okay. I had become trapped in a narcissistic trait pattern called love bombing. Our love was far from perfect. There were lies, secrets, and issues developing in our relationship that I ignored since regarding them would have destroyed the perfect image of the love I was longing for.

> Love bombing is an attempt to influence another person with over-the-top displays of attention and affection.
>
> *PSYCHOLOGY TODAY*

This is not to be confused with honest and heartfelt gifts presented during courtship or even in a marriage. Unlike love bombing, gift giving is usually a kind gesture and comes with the genuine intention of making the other person happy without any thoughts of what this gift will yield in return.

LOVE BOMBING—EXPLAINED BY PROFESSIONALS

There are many articles written about this subject, which leads me to believe that love bombing occurs quite regularly in relationships with narcissistic people. It is often described as a *bait and hook* agenda of the narcissist by at first being attentive, caring, and giving, and then at some point becoming less nice and kindhearted toward their partner. The purpose is to mask imperfections of the love bomber and the relationship.

I pulled a lot of good information from a website by *The Mind Journal* where I found this quote quite fitting:

"Manipulative people would never directly attack you. Rather, they would play with your emotions. Their tendency will be to make you do things which will benefit them. They will try to have you under their control in such a way that you will justify their dominance yourself."

In this article as well as others, it becomes clear that this form of manipulation is usually invisible in covert narcissism since the tail end of the love bombing doesn't end up in a loud argument or yelling (as it would in overt narcissism). It often slows down and almost disappears until it surfaces again when there is a need (e.g., when a lie was discovered) for the narcissist to remind the partner of their generosity. Therefore, love bombing is a trait that is found at the very beginning of a relationship but also resurfaces frequently to refresh the impression that they are exemplary companions. In both cases—overt and covert—the love bomber may appear with a gift in their hand or a romantic getaway weekend, assuring the partner that things will be okay and that things will be different from there on out.

The following explains it all quite well in the same article of *The Mind Journal*:

> *"A love bomber will say all the right things, and it'll just feel like you truly know him within days or weeks. [...] This will lead to the inevitable next step—he starts mirroring you; that is, he will start 'reflecting back to you' exactly what you really want to hear. This is because, by becoming your ideal man, he gains a tiny bit of control over you."*

I also learned from this article that as humans, we have a need to be loved and to feel good about ourselves. It is easy to see why love bombing is such an easy tool for narcissists to use on their prey, as they are quite skilled in finding those people that are especially responsive to this type of attention. While looking for a prospect to boost their own ego like a trophy, they seek those with temporarily low self-esteem due to personal or financial low points in their life.

The love-bombed partner is unaware and simply responds contentedly, as a void in their life is filled. Admiring and giving attention to their partner in times of need ensures the narcissist remains in control in the future. Once they feel a negative response from their partner due to the exposure of lies, secrets, or other destructive behavior, they use love bombing to get the love-needy partner to forgive quickly to earn that feeling of being loved back. The love-bombed partner over time will feel exhausted and drained by this emotional tug-of-war, not realizing where the exhaustion is coming from.

TAKEAWAY

Not everyone that likes to spoil their partner has bad intentions. Be assured that there are more honest and humble people than those that love bomb to manipulate. Nevertheless, there are hidden red flags to be aware of when getting involved with anyone that seems all too perfect right from the start. If you find them, reevaluate these "perfect" moments in your relationship to ensure that boundaries are not overstepped.

Did you notice the red flags of narcissistic traits in my story? The strongest one was love bombing, but there were others:

☑ Love bombing—"A Porsche for our first Valentine's"
Giving someone a car just one month after meeting that person is not normal. It left me feeling "cornered," but I brushed it off thinking he must just like me that much. I felt like I owed him and needed to be thankful.

☑ Rushing into intimacy—"We should move in together right away."
This can be absolutely okay for some couples, but it could also serve the purpose of controlling a partner or making them feel committed right from the start.

☑ Wearing a mask—"He is the perfect guy!"

As I read in an article of *Kids in The House*, there are many different masks. This one would be to "delight and impress you in any way that they can." And he sure knew how to impress.

☑ Soulmate scam artists and mirroring—"I just know we belong together."

"We have so much in common!" Perfectly said by the *Narcissist Abuse Support* website, "Having so much in common, because they mirror back to you your interests and passions, likes and dislikes, it makes it hard not to see how truly amazing it is that you are so compatible."

There is that old saying, "If it seems too good to be true, it probably is."

This applies in a relationship as well. Deep intimacy and becoming soulmates takes time and work. Think of your best friend. Chances are your friendship did not happen instantly. It took time and effort. And the same goes for romantic relationships.

You probably have specific hopes and dreams for your relationship. The love bomber, thanks to amazing listening skills, will wear the mask of the hero in your life. They will fulfill your wishes, make you feel adored, give you compliments, and even show *pretend empathy* to sucker you into their web. As a result, you become emotionally dependent on their "good behavior," willing to forgive anything bad they may do in between the rotations of soulmate and their "evil" other half.

If you are at the early stage of a relationship and these examples sound familiar, then you may be the victim of love bombing. Be mindful of his reactions and make sure you do not fall victim to thinking that an angry outburst or any other out of line behavior needs to be overlooked. Don't excuse it with the fact that he is "usually" the best guy ever. Countless gifts do *not* excuse unhealthy, abusive, hurtful, or otherwise immoral behavior.

WHAT ARE THE OPTIONS

If you are already way past this point and now realize that your love and devotion have been silently manipulated by your partner through love bombing, maybe even for years or decades, consider the following:

- Understand that the idea that they are your "soulmate" is just an illusion. They have not changed in the past; they are not going to change in the future. Staying with them means you accept their faults.
- If you are not okay to live in this pretend-to-be-perfect world, you need to prepare to leave that person once and for all—and as soon as possible.
- If you decide to leave, do so as soon as possible. Don't look back and stay strong. They will attempt to gain you back, as you were the perfect victim, and the void is destroying them. They will say anything, do anything, to get you back. They may even stalk or harass you. Telling them "no" is not acceptable to them. And even a little contact will open opportunities for them to push those buttons that worked in the past to get you back.

- Then, get your life back. Reconnect with friends you may have neglected while serving them. Check in with your family, let them know how important they are in your life. Fill them in on the basics. Ask them to be your account-ability people so you don't give in when your partner pleads.

While I remember feeling loved and adored, I also recall feeling a bit uncomfortable with the value of his gifts. I brushed it off as my own insecurity, as I had always had to tightly budget my funds and never in my life had been this spoiled by anyone. For in the future, I have learned to observe the giver's reaction. Are they excited to see me happy about a gift or does it feel like they are just waiting for praise for being kind? Is it about my reaction or how it makes *them* feel?

A red flag would be raised if, for example, they tell you all the troubles they went through, how much it cost, or how special it is. There is no definite answer as to whether specific instances are love bombing or humble giving, but feel free to use your gut feeling.

In my story, the fact that eighteen months went by without a fight didn't raise a red flag to me. And why should it, right? Isn't fighting a bad thing? At first glance, sure. But when you think about it, what are the chances that two people never fight in such a long period of time? I fight with my kids, my friends, even my besties. Not all the time, and not over trivial things, but it happens, and it feels okay. It seems that my relationships with them have grown more intimate, deeper, and stronger after a fight. A heated argument doesn't have to be ugly. It can remain respectful, simply serving the purpose of voicing different opinions or maybe releasing some hidden feelings that have been kept inside.

I found valuable information about "healthy arguments" on the marriage.com website if you are interested in finding out more about how to fight in a respectful way, promote trust, learn from disagreements, and even argue effectively in your marriage. My favorite is where the site says fighting "Encourages Communication: Feeling comfortable discussing any grievances that are bothering you means that you are in a safe and loving relationship. What could be better? When you know that you can discuss anything under the sun, good or bad, with your partner, that's a sign of true love."

MOVING FORWARD

I hope for my readers that this chapter has helped you learn the difference between love-based giving and love bombing. Keep your eyes open to see clearly whether gifts are of a loving nature or are a tool to manipulate and lead you to ignore the faulty areas in a relationship.

Moving right along, did I mention that there actually were a few imperfections in the perfect little world of Lester and me?

These were things like lies and secrets. Small or big, I forgave and forgot each and every one of them. Well—I forgave. Obviously, I didn't forget. I just didn't want to face them at the time. Ignoring them seemed to mask them into nonexistence.

Let's start with the biggest lie, and probably the one where I should have walked away. I was already too deprived of an objective perceptive at that time and so in love with my otherwise perfect man.

Let me throw a little surprise at you. Ready?

Lester and his eighty-year-old mom were drug peddlers for many years.

See what I mean? Leaves you with a big "Huh?" doesn't it?

Read all the nitty-gritty details in the next chapter.

CHAPTER 4

WHEEL OF FORTUNE

___

BACKGROUND STORY

THE BIG REVEAL

In our perfect little world, the days had become a smooth routine. Lester was working at the casino during the week, and three out of four weekends, he was gone with his mother on his drives to California to do his other job as a high-paid audio installer. I really would only have one weekend out of the month with him. I was okay with that at first, but as time went on, not being with him as much as I wanted began to bother me.

Eventually, there came a time when I felt like something was seriously off but just couldn't put my finger on it. Eighteen months had gone by since he first told me about his lucrative side gig. He and Kathy would leave on Fridays, he'd work on cars on Saturdays, and then be home by Sunday morning to go back to his security job in the afternoon. We talked or texted quite a bit while he was gone. I remember thinking he was such a hard worker. In our conversations on the phone, he would tell me what car he was working on, even giving me details as to what equipment he was adding or installing at that moment. I would have to hold for a moment here and there as he finished a particular task.

The truth is, I started to feel left out. *We share everything else, so why can't we share these drives to California?* I wondered. One weekend I finally asked him whether I could come along and if his mom could stay home. *Surely it must be hard on her,* I thought. He gave me the reason that Kathy in fact enjoyed the trips and that she liked to use the time to go shopping at the local mall. As to why they didn't fly rather than drive, he said they'd still have to rent a car anyhow since it was not near an airport. Plus, his mom liked driving much better than flying. She actually hated flying, he'd say.

After all this time though, I really wanted to go on a trip with him, so I insisted. I hinted that I was afraid he had another woman in another city, even joking that he could be living another life as I'd seen in the movies. It was then that we almost got into our first fight because I wouldn't let off. I demanded that either I get to go with him, or he give a legitimate reason as to why I couldn't come along.

His face changed from being angry to rather afraid and worried. He lowered his eyes, avoiding eye contact, and his whole body started trembling. He was stepping from one foot to the other, his index fingers nervously tapping his thumbs.

* * *

"Listen, there is something I guess I need to tell you about me," he said with a shaky voice. "And if you decide to turn around and walk away, I understand."

My stomach turned, as I had no idea what to expect. I was kidding when I mentioned him living another life. Now I was afraid of what I would hear next. Then again, I was so in love with him, I couldn't imagine that there was anything that would be bad enough for me to leave him. *How terrible could it be?* I thought. To me, he was the kindest, most caring man I had ever met.

After I took a seat on top of the kitchen counter, he continued, still avoiding my eyes. "On Thursday nights, when I say I go visit with mom, I actually go to a guy's house. His name is Lonnie. I count the money that he collects from his clients, and then I bundle it. On Fridays, me and Mom drive to northern Cali; that part is true. Except when we get there, we spend the night at a hotel." He took a deep breath before he continued. "Then in the morning, we drive a little farther up north, pick up marijuana in exchange for the money, then put it in sealed plastic bags in the trunk, and drive back home. There, now you know."

I felt sick to my stomach. I couldn't believe what I had just heard. It took me a moment to grasp what had just happened. I thought of all those times he'd told me on the phone how he was working on cars and chatted about the details of audio installations. None of that was true? None of it? It was all made up? He went on with more details. Apparently, he did in fact work in that profession in the past, prior to moving to Las Vegas, as well as for a few months after until he accepted the security job at the resort, but the story about the job in Northern California was made up.

"Didn't you think I deserved to know?" I asked after I mumbled a few words, still in disbelief, still trying to swallow the truth.

"I didn't want you to know about it because I didn't want you to worry," he said, still fumbling timidly with his fingers. "I had to do something to get me and Mom out of the mess we got ourselves in many years ago. And it's not something you tell a girl when you first meet. And I'd become so numb to this weekly routine and the stories that go along with it that I didn't even think about telling you. There was no point; we were fine. And I didn't want to lose you." Minutes went by without a word from either of us.

"I know I am asking a lot when I ask for you to please not leave me. I wouldn't blame you if you decided you don't love me enough to stick around. I'm so sorry. I didn't mean to hurt you. I love you, Micha."

* * *

With this apology and the sweetness in his voice, I started to feel bad for him. Surely this was all his mom's doing. There was no way he would betray me like this by his own will. She was the hateful one. He was always nothing but kind and loving, right? Here he was, risking getting caught just to provide for himself and his mother—and now for me as well.

My stomach churned when I realized that I had been enjoying life to the fullest—sponsored and paid for by drug deals. *What if my kids find out? What if he gets caught? Oh, my goodness, how can his mother support him with this? What kind of a mother-son relationship is this that they are accomplices in committing a crime together like Bonnie and Clyde?* So many questions filled my thoughts.

Then I remembered a time at a restaurant when she joked with him saying "You and me, we are gangsters!" sounding almost cute with her Hungarian accent. It had never even crossed my mind that she was actually speaking an honest word. I'd just laughed her comment off back then. They really *were* gangsters?

He didn't tell me how much they actually made with this side gig. The clothes he wore were far from fancy, and while she had outdated classy brand-name clothing in her closet, her favorite clothes were sweats and T-shirts. *Where did all the money go?* I had noticed that she was the one taking care of everything financially. She kept a ledger with expenses, bills, due dates, etc., and anytime he needed money, he would ask her for approval. When I asked him about that, he assured me it was his money, but she was pretty much in charge of how it was spent. He didn't seem to care as long as she supplied him with money when he needed funds. This explained where the money came from to pay for things like the little Porsche that he bought me right after we met. I hadn't worried about it at the time because it had made sense that he earned good money with audio installation on expensive cars.

I figured a great part of the money must have gone toward Kathy's never-ending renovations around the house. Lester did not have much control over her decisions there either, he said. Wood floor replaced the carpet, new molding was put around the ceilings, and many other projects were done. And all of them were taken care of by the same maintenance guy. This handyman must have made a nice monthly income with just the things they had him do—everything from hanging a picture to painting the house to the upkeep of the yard work. But it made sense to me now. They wouldn't want to hire multiple people or businesses if they could pay just one person—under the table.

* * *

In any case, I had to make a choice. I loved him too much and just didn't see myself giving up on him. *It's got to be his big heart that would drive him to do something crazy like this. Up to now, we haven't even had a fight—not even an argument!* I thought. Never even having a quarrel with him gave me the assurance that Lester was the good guy while Kathy must have been the one driving him to do things—even illegal things—to make her happy.

Almost instantly and without giving it much thought, I knew I would stay by his side. I offered to stay but that he would have to help me build up my wellness business enough to relieve him from this terrible side-gig. Surely it wasn't he who truly wanted this, and I was certain that I didn't want to lose him. Leaving was not an option. Then I promised him I would work really hard to free him from this burden as soon as possible. I felt so very bad for him that my heart was hurting.

From that day forward, we hardly ever talked about his weekend trips. I started to tell others the same lies he told me. All that time, whenever anyone asked me what he did for a living, I'd reply, "He drives with his mom to Northern California and works on high-dollar cars." That seemed to satisfy their questions about where all the money was coming from. I learned to leave it at that to protect my husband.

"But love is blind, and lovers cannot see the pretty follies that themselves commit."

—WILLIAM SHAKESPEARE

WHAT WAS I THINKING?

I wonder today, *what I was thinking?* How could I stay with a man who would commit crimes to cheat himself into a nice lifestyle? I despise lies and have always believed in being truthful. Yet, I let Lester—who I was living with for nearly eighteen months—get by all while he pretended he was a genuine and hardworking man. Why? Haven't honesty and trust always been a must for me in any relationship? How could I have been so blind to reality? How could I neglect my own values?

"It always comes down to one thing. It's all about the money!" was one of Lester's favorite quotes. And now I know that he actually meant that, word for word. Taking this a step further, his apparent inability to handle challenges was obviously motivation to even commit a crime, producing the money he needed to buy his way out of problem situations and into the feeling of having freedom, control, and happiness in life.

And me? I literally bought right into this huge lie and excused this unethical behavior by blaming the mother. Without thinking, I adopted his feeling of being entitled to a better lifestyle, as I had been short on money for all my life. I allowed myself to live with the knowledge of his underhand dealing and continued to live a lavish lifestyle, receive gifts, go out to eat, watch movies and shows, and have the assurance that bills would be taken care of.

With my constant focus on being an understanding and supportive girlfriend and later a wife, I missed the fact that I lived in betrayal of my own moral principles.

MY RESEARCH

According to NPD expert Sam Vaknin, who wrote *Malignant Self-Love: Narcissism Revisited*, money serves as a substitute for love that has been lacking in a MEM's life from early on in childhood. The substitution of love with money shows in adulthood by the way they handle and worship it. They develop a sense of entitlement that leads them to think they should be part of other people's earnings. Their feelings of being superior show in their belief they deserve more money than they have. As a result, a narcissist tends to live life beyond their means, run up credit cards on endless shopping sprees, enjoy gambling, and may even become a substance abuser.

Vaknin also describes narcissists as being irresponsible and shortsighted, as they hope for magical solutions and protection from negative outcomes. This would explain why they often end up in financial ruin, seeking ways out like committing financial crimes or pestering friends and family for support. The more they fantasize about their imaginary wealth, the more they end up spending in a greedy love-hate relationship with money. Their attitude toward money is essentially what creates a mental cycle of conflict between how impressive they think they are and what little power they possess.

My favorite findings in Sam Vaknin's focus on narcissists and money are the following quotes, as I have stood witness to each:

- "Money shields him from life itself, from the outcomes and consequences of his actions; it insulates him warmly and safely, like a benevolent blanket, like a mother's goodnight kiss."
- "Money has little to do with the narcissist's actual physical needs or even with his social interactions. The narcissist leverages lucre to acquire status or to impress others."
- "Most narcissists conceal the true extent of their wealth, hoard it, accumulate it."
- "Narcissists are not necessarily tight-fisted, though. Many narcissists spend money on restaurants and trips abroad and books and health products. They buy gifts though reluctantly and as a maintenance chore."
- "Narcissists addictively gamble and speculate and lose fortunes. But he does all this not for the love of money,

for he does not use it to gratify himself or to cater to his needs. It is the power that it bestows on him that matters."

TAKEAWAY

Lester and Kathy's poor sense of money and finances was a constant all throughout their life. Way back when his dad died, his mom took the life insurance money, bought an old house, and as I mentioned before, spent nearly a fortune on renovating every inch of it. Then they sold it for a $200,000 profit but still ended up filing for bankruptcy a few years after they bought the house in Las Vegas. Their lavish lifestyle was way beyond their means, and the countless credit cards and store credits became a problem. Even after their financial ruin, they kept overspending on a sparse income, and when the opportunity was presented to him to make "easy" money delivering drugs, he took it. Spending less and adjusting their budget to his regular income seemed to present too many challenges, while ten thousand dollars or more a month sounded much simpler.

By the way, none of the earnings from the side-gig ever reflected in the value of the house. According to Kathy's carefully kept ledger of their criminal expenses, it added up to over a million dollars' worth of delivered drugs over the years. They neither saved money to create an emergency or retirement fund, nor did they invest any of it into the equity of the home. If this sounds mind-blowing, you are right. It blew my mind too when I found out a lot of numeric details at the end of our marriage after having worked for an honest income for all my life. I had been a single mother of four children many years back and never had any understanding of wasteful living by those who can't afford it.

How did I not see all this? Living large was definitely not my thing. But that was exactly what suckered me into this dream of being carefree. I was so blindly in love that I did not even see the red flags of lies, deceit, money worshipping, etc. And because of this dysfunctional relationship, I neglected my own moral principles more and more. Honesty and truth were out the window.

* * *

Obsessive gambling, as it turns out, is also a sign to look for in narcissists. And I am sure that is even more important when living in Las Vegas. When I was with him, I enjoyed playing here and there for twenty bucks. But apparently there was a lot more to it that I didn't know of; I didn't find out until I went through paperwork before I moved out. And while I knew he liked to gamble a lot more than I did, I did not know he was a regular at Dottie's, a local chain bar that was all over town. I found an annual summary sheet from the year he had his accident showing well over two hundred thousand dollars won across forty nine taxable winnings in one year, which translates into hundreds and hundreds of attempts and *a lot* of hours of gambling to hit *just one* large winning. Lester said he used this income in his tax return to offset the money he earned with his drug deliveries. It made sense—at the time. But I was not aware that he was gambling excessively.

And mind you, according to the stack of payout stubs I found, it was only two weeks after his release from the hospital with a severe brain injury that he went right back to Dottie's. That's just four weeks after waking up from an induced coma that his mind was clear enough to remember to go hit up the slot machines. I call this pretty obsessive.

In church, I learned that with God being the creator of all, he is also the creator of money. The Bible talks a great deal about it, and according to *biblemoneymatters.com,* there are well over two thousand verses about money.

The one that says it clearest to me on how to put hope into wealth is Matthew 6:24 (New International Version), "No one can serve two masters. Either you will hate the one and love the other, or you will be devoted to the one and despise the other. You cannot serve both God and money." I have also learned in church that we the people are the managers of money; we don't actually own it. Living by this principle gives me great respect for not only every dollar earned but also every dollar spent.

In addition to this, even the church teaches me to obey the law. The Bible speaks decisively on this issue. Romans 13:1-2 (NIV) says, "Submission to Governing Authorities. Let everyone be subject to the governing authorities, for there is no authority except that which God has established. The authorities that exist have been established by God. Consequently, whoever rebels against the authority is rebelling against what God has instituted, and those who do so will bring judgment on themselves."

* * *

I hope this chapter helped you understand how narcissists feel about money and will help others identify the hidden red flags in a relationship pointing toward signs of unhealthy behavior.

While my opinions may be partially based on Christian beliefs, I don't think many would support Lester's statement that "It is okay to break the law to get rich quickly and easily, as long as no one actually gets hurt," when expressing his attitude toward delivering drugs to make money. He didn't consider himself a criminal. "It's not like I'm robbing banks," he'd say.

If you feel like your spouse, partner, or loved one idolizes money to the point of worshiping it, you have reason to be concerned. I think many agree that not having money can be a problem and having it can solve problems. Being wealthy is a dream for many people and is not bad in and of itself. But I am talking about an unhealthy and obsessive want for fortune regardless of casualties or loss of friendships. If you are around someone like that, you want to make sure that you don't get suckered into actions that go against your honorable standards. When in a relationship with a narcissist who regularly manipulates your own beliefs, this can easily happen without you even noticing.

MOVING FORWARD

Life continued to be "perfectly fine," with all its usual imperfections, those forgivable "little" lies about his visits to his mom's and other minor interruptions in our happy life. Even the bigger ones were forgiven and forgotten. All I saw through my rosy glasses was that I'd finally made it. I had the husband of my dreams, and we were living our perfect life in our little happy place.

That is, until one day in July of 2015—the day that changed our world forever. It was just half a year after we'd gotten married that I received a phone call from the medical center in downtown Las Vegas. Lester had been in a very bad car accident on one of his drug runs.

What came next is what turned out to be the beginning of the end of our perfect little world.

It was going to get worse than I could even imagine.

A lot worse.

CHAPTER 5

TRAUMATIZED

"The paradox of trauma is that it has both the power to destroy and the power to transform and resurrect."

—*PETER A. LEVINE*

BACKGROUND STORY

THE DAY OF HIS ACCIDENT

It was late afternoon on Saturday, July 25, 2015—just six months after Lester and I had gotten married.

I knew that Lester and his mom were on their way back from their usual trips to California as he had texted me early that morning. Going by what time it was, he should have made it to Las Vegas by early that afternoon. Right about the time I expected him home, a call came from the hospital letting me know that Lester had been in a really bad car accident.

They asked me to come in right away if I wanted to see him, as he was about to go in for brain surgery.

I was scared and my mind went numb as I was fearing the worst. I grabbed my car keys and wallet and tried not to cry as I had to drive almost thirty minutes to get to the hospital. On the way, I was preoccupied with a million questions.

He must have wrecked here in Vegas, I thought. Then I wondered where his mom was. *How about her? Was she okay? Was she injured as well?* I was worried about Kathy. Regardless of how much she disliked me, I hoped she was okay. *If she is okay, why didn't she call me? Surely, she would have phoned me to let me know about an accident. So maybe she's hurt also?*

When I got to the ER, the medical staff had already prepared Lester for the operation. While he seemed unconscious, I assured him that he was going to be okay and that I would be there when he came out of surgery. I kissed him on the forehead and then had to let him go as they wheeled him through the double doors. There I was, devastated and helpless, as there was nothing I could do other than to go back into the waiting area. That's where I saw Kathy and her and Lester's friends. She seemed fine, not a scratch on her. I went over to where she was and asked her what had happened.

She got up out of her seat, came even closer to me, and screamed in my face, "You are the devil in my son's life! It is all your fault!" Her thin index finger stabbed my chest as her stale breath barraged my face. Her face was only inches away from mine when she tried to reach out and hit me while a friend of hers pulled her back. I felt tears shooting into my eyes. Figuring out what had happened to my husband was all I could think about—that and why Kathy could possibly be so angry with me. I was so confused about the whole situation. It seemed the world was falling apart right in front of me. *Why am I the devil, and how is it all my fault?*

The waiting area of the emergency room was well lit by large windows along one wall. My mother-in-law took back her seat on the opposite side of where I sat. She was surrounded by their friends who showed no sign of concern with how I was doing. It was like I wasn't even there. Whenever they did look over to where I sat, I could feel the hate radiating from their gazes.

My heart was beating hard, and I felt my throat closing, making it hard to swallow. My forehead was hurting from furrowing so much, and my eyes wanted to let the tears out, but confusion seemed to work like a barrier against their release.

I sat there, waiting for a doctor or a nurse to deliver updates on Lester. All I knew was that Lester and Kathy had been in a wreck, he was in surgery for a brain bleed and in critical condition, and Kathy blamed everything on me. Where, when, why, how—nobody would tell me anything, and my head was spinning trying to figure it all out. All I had was Lester's phone in my hands and his angry mother sitting across from me in the ER waiting room.

A text on his phone indicated the accident happened around 11:00 a.m. but also showed two hours of him having conversations afterward but nothing sent to me. So, he was okay after the wreck but no call, no text to me? Nothing made sense.

Why were their friends here with Kathy while I was alone? Why did I get a call from the hospital and not from Lester or Kathy? I was so very lost and confused. Why did he not contact me? Why didn't she or anyone else? Did they hate me that much? What have I done to him or any of them to not even deserve a call when my husband nearly died? Now I was there while my beloved husband was fighting for his life, and nobody would talk to me. Kathy's anger didn't surprise me. She never did like me from the moment she first met me. But why Lester? Why his friends?

Then I went right back to the painful question: why didn't Lester call me? I was his wife! For two hours, he texted and called others. Should I not have gotten a call before anyone else? I thought I was the most important person in his life; he had said so himself. So why didn't he call me?

MORE THAN A PERSON SHOULD ENDURE

The next two days were some of the most stressful days of my entire life. And the weeks to follow were the darkest days I have ever gone through. I have never felt that alone and lost. The things I had to deal with while he was in the hospital were almost too much for one person to handle. I don't even know how I managed. Looking back, it is all just a blur. I am pretty sure I was on autopilot for most of the time. Thankfully, I kept a journal during that time. And instead of rewriting and trying to make it all into a neat narrative, I will add it at the end of this book for you to relive the pains and struggles as they happened with me. You may get a deeper understanding of what added to my struggles during this dreadful time.

As I found out days later, during the accident, he lost control of the vehicle, ran off the road, and hit his head hard enough to cause bleeding inside the brain. This explained at least why he was doing well enough for a couple of hours to make those phone calls. He had his mother, who did not sustain any injuries, taken home by friends, and the car was also picked up quickly by another guy to hide the weed that was stowed in the trunk. It seems that he had sense enough to take care of his illegal business but didn't even think of notifying me about the crash. After some time, he started feeling dizzy, a helicopter was called by the police that had arrived, and he was flown to the closest trauma center which happened to be in Las Vegas. None of this explained why Lester did not notify me.

Lester made it through the brain surgery as well as could have been expected. He stayed in an induced coma for two weeks to give his brain time to heal. They removed part of his skull to allow room for the brain to swell. Once they reduced the sedation, his recovery progressed well, and within just six weeks, he was released from the hospital. His speech and comprehension were fine, but he was still very much like a child in his limited ability to process his surroundings appropriately. Due to a lack of protection of his brain, he was required to always wear a fitted helmet until further notice. He was ordered to rest, was not allowed to drive or to perform physically straining activities like lifting or running for the time being.

Everything that happened after this was nothing short of an emotional roller coaster filled with events that I wouldn't wish on my worst enemy. We went through more challenges over the coming six years than most couples experience in a lifetime. To tell each of the stories in detail would be enough to write a whole new book. So, allow me to summarize some of the most impactful ones in just a few paragraphs to give you a glance at a few of the things we dealt with:

After bringing Lester home from the hospital, he asked to spend time with his mom, as she had stopped coming to the hospital after the first few weeks. Because of Lester's child-like behavior and his mother's hateful attitude toward me, I was afraid she would influence Lester's feelings about me. I agreed for him to visit for a few hours, hoping it would do no harm. After five hours, she dropped him back off at our house. Something was different about him. He was keeping his distance and hardly spoke with me. When I tried to talk to him, he responded as if he were worried that I would hit him. I feared something had been said while he was at his mother's. Something she had said must have made him scared of me.

Torn between trying to figure out what it was that was bothering him and having to go back to work a few days later, I left the house early in the morning to work at our wellness store. The last two months had taken their toll on the business so much that by that time, it'd lost most of its clientele. With all the money invested into it, I did not want to lose the business, and we needed income. With Lester not able to work, our financial situation was at risk. On my second day at the store, I couldn't get a response from Lester via text or call. I had a bad feeling about this and left about midafternoon. When I got home, Lester was gone and so were many of his clothes, bathroom toiletries, and other personal belongings.

I didn't understand. My heart was racing. I was beyond worried. Did something happen to him? Was he okay? I wondered if Kathy knew anything.

KATHY STOLE MY HUSBAND!

I drove to his mother's house and rang the bell but got no answer. Through the glass door, I could see Kathy and Lester back in the kitchen. I started knocking, but they obviously ignored me. I called the non-emergency number for the police, hoping they would help me to get my husband back. While waiting for their arrival, I sat in the car, crying. I couldn't believe that my mother-in-law had taken advantage of the incoherent Lester to fulfill her own desire to have her son all to herself. After the police showed up and spent an hour or so inside the house, they came out. The word was that this was where Lester lived. Apparently, Lester had told them he did not live with me, did not want to be with me, and that we were going through a divorce. I was advised Lester appeared to be of sound mind and to know what he was saying, so there was nothing they could do. All my pleading about his injury led nowhere, as he was not even wearing his helmet anymore. I had no choice but to leave him where he was. Devastated and feeling helpless, I went home and cried myself to sleep.

The next few days I did all I could to figure out his whereabouts. Since I had access to all his online accounts, I was able to track a lot of what was happening. I was shocked to find out that just days after he went to his mom's, he was driving his car and even visiting his favorite bar where he likely went to gamble (years later, I found receipts of winnings confirming this). Many calls and texts showed up on our cellular account. He was making countless calls to the people that I despised—His college flame Jessica, as well as the main drug guy, Lonnie. Fearing the worst, my barely mended heart was being ripped into a thousand pieces, little by little, and there was nothing I could do. It felt like a slow death. Not knowing how he was doing with his brain unprotected was driving me crazy. He was driving his car, which he wasn't allowed to, acting as if nothing had happened to his head. I knew it all had to do with Kathy. I wondered if she was hoping for him to get back on the road to take care of the bills that remained unpaid, putting her comfortable lifestyle at risk. Could she be so selfish as to disregard his medical condition? Did he actually believe he was okay and back to normal? He must have, but I knew better. He was not okay.

PAINFUL MEMORIES
Written during the weeks of silence after Kathy stole Lester away from me.

"These days I spend my time preoccupied with work and errands to run, not even thinking about what goes on deep inside my heart. And then from one moment to another, I want to curl up into a ball. Tears shoot from my eyes, and I cry so hard that I forget the world around me. Thoughts of pain and anger overlap in my head, switching from one to the other, making me feel crazy. The pain from having lost my husband, my best friend, my soulmate. That sweet man that told me I was beautiful, giving me looks that let me know I was his queen. The man that adored me, head to toe with all my

faults, he who assured me that there was nothing that would ever come between us.

What happened to him? Where is he? Everything that I thought was true love is gone, lost in space. It all seems so backward. Usually, people wake up from a nightmare, drenched in sweat, still shaking from what they saw or felt in their dream. But this? Now? It is like I was suddenly ripped out of the most amazing dream where the world was all fuzzy and warm and I woke up into the nightmare. Like nothing that I remember is true, my world has fallen apart, and I am feeling nothing but hurt and pain in my heart.

I feel alone and broken. I cry and cry, my heart hurts and I keep hearing thoughts inside my head about missing my husband. Is this how grief feels, I wonder? Is this what it feels like when you lose a person unexpectedly? It must be. Will I ever see him again, feel him again, receive the kindness that made me feel loved the way he did? I feel so broken."

* * *

Weeks passed, and it felt like an eternity went by. I was so alone in our big home. And the wellness shop did not survive the financial crunch. I had to close its doors quite soon after the accident. I had no news about Lester until just before my birthday in September when he finally started to respond to my texts. My heart jumped out of my chest with every notification. By then, I had found a local call center job as a customer service representative for a worldwide travel agency. I was grateful, as it allowed me to pay my bills while trying to catch up on those that were already late for payment. Soon after, Lester and I started meeting up at our old home that I still lived in, and it felt like things were coming back to him. Feeling bad for what had happened, he promised to work things out with his mom and started coming over more often. We spent days and even nights together, and for a few weeks the world seemed almost perfect again.

THEIR TRIP TO HAWAII

It was a few months after his accident in October of 2015 when Lester told me that he and Kathy were going on a ten-day trip to Hawaii. I didn't like the idea. I also knew that nothing at this point was up to me; he was following his mother's wishes once again. She wanted to go to Hawaii to see her longtime friend Vanessa who had done accounting for them some ten years back. It seemed odd to me that they even went at all. Kathy didn't like to travel by plane but now did not seem to mind going on such a long flight.

While in Hawaii, Lester texted me frequently, telling me how much he enjoyed the scenery and the food but that on the other hand he was also bored and wanted to come home. I wanted him home too, as I missed him dearly. While there, we talked on the phone almost every evening, and he told me about the excursions he and his mom went on. I was also worried about him, knowing that neither he nor his mother were taking his brain injury seriously. Having flown in an airplane since I was little, I knew about the pressure a person feels in their head when taking off or landing. Everything seemed fine until midweek when I noticed that his speech had started to become slurred. He also stuttered and had trouble getting the words to come out right. It became worse every day, and by his return, he had lost the ability to speak completely.

Not only could he not talk but he also couldn't write. Thankfully, he still understood everything that was said to him. We went to see his neurologist who explained that this delayed loss of frontal lobe function could happen after this type of brain damage. There was a great chance that it was temporary, the doctor said. It took weeks for his speech to improve, but it never fully recovered. From that time forward, he was left with a slight speech impediment that caused him to have trouble finding the right words at times. I learned to deal with this quite easily, but he had a hard time accepting that he had become somewhat disabled. It must have crushed what little hope he had to get his life back on track. Consequentially, he started coming over less and less.

A few weeks later in November, I was home alone when a man rang the doorbell.

"Are you Michaela?" he asked.

"Yes, that's me." I replied.

"Ma'am, you've been served," he said, handing me an envelope. He then turned around and walked off.

I just stood there in disbelief. Had Lester really filed for divorce? I didn't understand. I'd thought we were working things out. He mentioned that I deserved better than to be with him; he even suggested for us to stay separated for a while. But divorce? I was so confused—again. We'd been doing so well! Or so I thought? I had told him I didn't want a divorce when he moved back to his mom's!

Two more months went by with us still spending time together, which didn't help my confusion. I did my best to convince him that he could still withdraw the petition. While insisting I was better off without him, he would nevertheless spend days and nights in a row with me at the house. His constant desire to be with me led me to think the divorce was not his idea. My fear was that Kathy was the one behind all this. I kept hoping for him to see how much we loved each other. Then in January, the mailman delivered a large envelope, certified return receipt requested. I opened it and pulled out a legal document. The divorce was final. I stared at the paper. So this was it? We date, we tell each other we love one another, but now we were divorced? It felt like my heart had stopped. I tried to call him, but he wouldn't answer. In the weeks to follow, I was a mess in all the ways possible: emotionally, physically, and spiritually. I felt broken.

Not being able to handle the financial responsibilities that came with the big house, I searched for a new place to start over in. By the end of February, the lease of our rental house had ended, and I had found a cute condo in an apartment complex about thirty minutes farther north of Lester's house. There I was in my new apartment. It was time to think of myself, and I was beginning to get my ambitions back. I renovated the place, decorated it with newly purchased items that I had found on sale, and made it my new home. The divorce was final, yes, but I couldn't stop thinking of Lester. Was this really the end? Or was there a chance to get him back?

I was not yet convinced that Lester truly believed this divorce was what he wanted. He still texted me daily, and we started to see each other again a few times a week. After a couple of months, it became clear that a court-issued piece of paper was not the solution to our problems. We loved each other still, and for the following year, we spent as much time together as we could. While he continued living with Kathy and I had my condo, I just knew that over time he would see how much I loved him. I just had to be patient.

MY RESEARCH

Looking back and writing down these memories hurts. I even cried while writing this chapter. It was so very painful and probably the most tumultuous time in my relationship with Lester. This chapter is relevant if you have ever found yourself in a painful situation that some would call "rock bottom."

According to *Psychology Today*, trauma is "a person's emotional response to a distressing experience." Knowing this is important, but understanding its significance is your doorway to healing.

Therefore, I want to talk about this before we go any further. It's important for you to know that events or happenings in your life can be so devastating and traumatizing that feeling lost and confused is your body's natural reaction to the shock. The emotional damage done is not to be taken lightly. I want to let you know that if you have suffered a traumatizing event at any time in your life, you need to address it in order to heal. Many of the stories that happened after Lester's accident were traumatizing in and of themselves. I believe that by not addressing them and trying to be the strong wife, it created a domino effect that led from one bad decision to another. My eyes were closed to reality due to—you got it—being traumatized.

WHAT TRAUMATIZED MEANS TO ME

Trauma is just like a physical injury, except it's mental. The damage is done to your psyche and your well-being, and your brain reacts like the rest of the body when going through an extremely painful injury; it goes into shock. This happens to protect the body from both physical and emotional injuries because humans are not designed to endure pain beyond a certain level. This state of shock explains feelings like numbness, lifelessness, and emptiness. Your body refuses to feel the pain and tries to protect you. But like a physical wound, just because it's numb doesn't mean there was no damage. When you're injured, an open wound must be treated to prevent getting infected. If transferred to the context of a psychological injury, it too must be treated gently and freed of anything that could make things worse.

In my case, having to deal with the way Lester's mother and friends treated me after his accident while trying to deal with him almost dying and having remaining brain damage was overwhelming. What came after was like pouring dirt into an open wound and rubbing it in. The event of the accident was traumatizing, and those that followed over the years didn't leave room for healing. The pain became too much to endure, leading me to become numb to reality.

Knowing this allows me to look back without feeling guilty or ashamed for not being able to see all the things that were wrong in our relationship that now seem so obvious. I stopped blaming myself for making bad decisions that lead to the same mistakes over and over.

HOW PROFESSIONALS DEFINE TRAUMA

According to studies by the National Center for Biotechnology Information, it has been shown that about 60–75 percent of individuals in North America experience a traumatic event at some point in their lifetime.

I found a brief and great definition on the website of the National Center for Biotechnology Information:

What is emotional and psychological trauma?

Emotional and psychological trauma is the result of extraordinarily stressful events that shatter your sense of security, making you feel helpless in a dangerous world. Psychological trauma can leave you struggling with upsetting emotions, memories, and anxiety that won't go away. It can also leave you feeling numb, disconnected, and unable to trust other people.

Traumatic experiences often involve a threat to life or safety, but any situation that leaves you feeling overwhelmed and isolated can result in trauma, even if it doesn't involve physical harm. It's not the objective circumstances that determine whether an event is traumatic, but your subjective emotional experience of the event. The more frightened and helpless you feel, the more likely you are to be traumatized.

Then regarding how we respond, I learned on the website Medical News Today that people who have gone through trauma might experience a wide variety of feelings like rejection, anger, fear, gloom, embarrassment, bewilderedness, numbness, guilt, shame, hopelessness, or impatience. It also talks about how a person may become secluded and have nightmares or even unexplained outbreaks of aggression. Physically, they may experience headaches, digestive issues, exhaustion, excessive perspiration, and feelings of distress, as well as having trouble falling or staying asleep. In some cases, the victims start showing symptoms such as depression, anxiety, and substance abuse.

TAKEAWAY

Bottom line: trauma is an injury and must be recognized as such. If gone undetected, it can make things worse.

When you find yourself in a situation that suddenly leaves you feeling in shock, alone, confused, or hurt, my personal advice is to seek emotional shelter by reaching out to close friends or family members. Their love and devotion to you will help you get over the initial pain and give you the necessary strength to take any next steps. While your mind is feeling empty and in shock, it is a good idea to follow the advice of your loved ones, as I can guarantee you, they see things clearer than you.

For those seeking additional help on how to deal with the effects of trauma, I highly recommend the website of helpguide.org, especially the solution-packed article called "Coping with Emotional and Psychological Trauma."

While I am thankful that I have loving friends who offered their support, I still found myself sinking deeper and deeper into the darkness of anger and depression. I felt lost and afraid. I needed more than their support; I needed the strength to move on and pull through.

It was at this time that a church I had driven by for years had a big sign on the side of the building that said, "Come As You Are." A week after the accident, I walked in on a Sunday morning. I cannot remember much of what happened since it all seems like a blur, but there were women who invited me to attend their weekly support group. It was there with the help of these ladies and their comfort and kindness that I was able to find this strength through their prayers and love for a stranger like me.

It wasn't necessarily what these women said, just the fact that they took me into their circle, loved me, and showed me that I was worthy of being loved. They showed me that whatever the source of my pain—betrayal, lies, and disloyalty—I would be okay. They told me that God would give me strength through faith. And they were right.

The Lord will keep you from all harm—he will watch over your life; the Lord will watch over your coming and going both now and forevermore.

PSALMS 121:7-8 (NIV)

Finding support is an absolute necessity to properly come out the other side of any traumatizing event. I found it in my church, but any other small group environment like friends, family, or even professional advice will do. I don't recommend trying to do it on your own.

- Know that feeling lost and confused during and after any traumatic event is normal. And yes, even emotional abuse in any form is traumatizing.
- It is okay to start talking to people you trust about your hurt and feelings. They may not have all the answers, but they will be able to make you feel heard and loved.
- Create plenty of comforting moments to give you a peaceful experience. This could be a long bath with candles, a stroll in the park, an inspiring movie while cuddling up in your blanket, or maybe just listening to calming music.
- Get back to living your life! Get back into your routines as quickly as possible. Focusing on important and positive things will help your healing process.
- Just like after a physical injury, you need to take good care of your body. Have plenty of rest, good nutrition, and an overall healthy active lifestyle.

- Seek therapy—it really helps! You can start by joining local support groups, maybe visit a local church. They often offer programs to help with healing.
- And lastly, be patient. What you have gone through is *major*. There is no shortcut to healing. There will be triggers that make you relive the pain, burst out in tears, or curl up in a ball. Know it takes time to heal. You will be okay.

MOVING FORWARD

There are quite a few sayings floating around on the internet about relationship issues, and one of them said something like...

"If you find yourself surfing the internet to figure out someone's behavior, that's probably a red flag you don't want to ignore."

I wish I had read these wise words when I felt early on that something was off in our relationship, and I started researching. One of the issues I always wondered about early on was Lester's habit of lying. It was more than once that I would tell a friend, "My husband is perfect, except for those lies! I don't think he trusts me enough to be honest with me, but I have never lied to him, so I don't know where that is coming from!"

Remembering the countless times he lied to me, there are a few that stick out. While I was numb to his daily lies, there were big ones that each were enough by themselves for a woman to have reason to just walk away.

Today I think of them and just shake my head. Why in the world didn't I see that nothing ever changed?

You will know what I mean after reading the next chapter.

CHAPTER 6

LIES, LIES, AND MORE LIES

———

*Question: "How do you know
if a narcissist is lying?"*

Answer: "When his lips are moving!"

—ANONYMOUS

BACKGROUND STORY

At some point after Lester had confessed to his drug deliveries, it seemed that I had become part of the "other" life that Lester and Kathy had been living for many years. They went on their weekend trips to California to drop off money and pick up weed, and I had learned to not only live with the lie but also tell it to others if asked. And since we were not married, I didn't see that it was my place to tell him what he should or should not do.

Our love life was like before though, the closest thing to perfect—if you ignore all the constant little lies that got him out of telling the truth, usually when he went to see his mom and didn't want me to know. "I didn't want you to get upset," was his standard explanation. I started to slowly believe that these lies were okay, as they didn't really harm anything.

When his lies got a little bigger, I allowed my love for him to put blinders on my eyes. I knew if I got upset over the untruths or half-truths or untold events, I would make him feel like he had betrayed me, and he assured me this wasn't the case. He once told me the reason he lied so frequently was that he had learned with his mother that "what she doesn't know won't hurt her," and so he applied it to us. He'd ask me to give it more time, tell me he would do his best not to do it again, or assure me the last thing he wanted to do was hurt me.

TRIP TO HOUSTON WITH HIS COLLEGE BUDDY—SUMMER OF 2014

Then a few weeks after he came back...

It had been just another day after coming home from work. While I was cooking supper, Lester came downstairs after his bath and casually asked me, "Hey, I wondered if it would be okay with you if I was to meet up with an old college buddy in Houston? We wanted to go have a few drinks, talk about the good old days. I'll only be gone for a few days."

"Sure, honey. You need to get away a little! I'm glad you guys get to meet up. I hope you have a great time," I replied.

We had been together for twenty months, and there was no doubt in my mind that this was a harmless get-together with one of his old friends from school. I was quite happy for him, as he didn't have many friends from the old days, and I thought he deserved to get away for a few days.

He called me from Texas to let me know that he'd made it okay and that his college buddy had picked him up. He said they were now on their way to go have a drink.

"Have one for me too!" I said, encouraging him to have a good time.

Later on, he sent me a cute picture standing in front of a brick wall next to a bar. It had a mural with "I love you" in huge letters. I loved that picture, as it showed me how much he thought of me even while with his friend.

Weeks later at a local event, we were sitting next to each other, and he was checking his phone. He was still getting used to smartphones. He had the habit of erasing most of the info on it and didn't keep many photos of anything either. I figured he thought using up space would slow down the phone. It kind of bothered me though, as I felt like he was hiding something, but I convinced myself that it was an old habit left over from his flip phone days. On top of that, we had always trusted each other with everything. There were no secrets between us, or so I thought. As he began to scroll through photos next to me, I noticed something.

"Wait, that's the picture you sent me when you were in Houston. There are more? Let me see!"

"You've already seen it," he said, quickly swiping the screen to get out of the photo album.

"But there are more. Who is that with you? Let me see!"

My anxiety rose as I spotted a woman standing next to him. A bit frustrated, I grabbed the phone out of his hand to look at it myself. I could tell he was annoyed and getting angry.

"Why would you take my phone from me?" he said.

I stared at the pictures that had not been deleted yet. There it was: the picture he had sent me—but then the following ones were with a girl next to him. He had his arm around her, and they both looked happy, wearing big smiles on their faces.

"I want to know who that is!" I demanded.

"You know her. It's Pookie, my college buddy. I told you I would meet up with her!"

"I thought you were meeting up with a guy! You never said it was gonna be Pookie! You never said 'he' or 'she' when we talked about it. Oh my gosh, how sneaky can you be?"

My heart was beating so fast. I could feel anger and betrayal flowing through my veins. I got up from my chair and ran toward the parking garage with him following me.

"You would have never let me go if you had known it was her! You don't like her, but she's my friend. Just like you have friends, but you don't like mine! You can't blame me for not telling you. I wanted to meet up with her, but I also didn't want to argue with you. That's why I didn't tell you."

I wasn't sure what to think. He'd spent a whole weekend with her. He'd spent nights at her apartment. They'd taken a picture arm in arm under the same "I love you" mural he had sent me. Although anger simmered at the edge of his voice, he assured me that nothing had happened between the two of them. And upon seeing how upset he was getting, I believed him. I figured it was my fault, that I was just blowing things out of proportion. I told myself it would be wrong of me to accuse him of something. That while yes, he left out the fact he was meeting his college flame, but if he said nothing happened, then nothing happened. He was definitely right to think that I wouldn't have let him leave to see another woman. I felt that maybe I was too possessive, and since his mother restricted his thoughts and actions for all his life, it was no wonder he would have secrets from me out of fear of being rejected.

Her name was Jessica, but he and his mom called her Pookie. I knew that he was somewhat obsessed with her ever since they'd met in college. He had a diary in which he wrote about her on and off for many years in his twenties, dreaming up a bright future with her while she never really showed interest in anything more than casual friendship. He had written down his fantasies about when she would finally fall deeply in love with him, how they would buy a house and have two children. He was very detailed in his writings about her. So yes, I felt it was reasonable to have concerns that there was more to this Houston trip.

I also knew that his mom really liked her. I could tell by the way Kathy talked about her, and I could see why. Jessica never stuck around, always kept her distance, and only reached out to Lester when she needed help or money. This time, Lester said she'd needed help with moving. Nothing serious, he assured me, just a longtime friend who needed help, and if he had told me, he would not have been able to help an old friend because of me. We left it at that. I thought about how right he was in his accusations that I would not have let him go. I ended up dropping the questioning, taking the blame for an unnecessary argument, and I asked him to forgive me for not trusting him.

TRIP TO HAWAII WITH KATHY IN OCTOBER 2015 – PART 1
Then a few weeks after he came back...

It was fall of 2015, a few months after the accident, and Lester was living with his mom, while I was still at our rental home. One evening in November, Lester and I decided to go out to eat on one of our casual dates. We'd just parked in front of a local Texas-style BBQ restaurant when his phone began to ring on the car's Bluetooth. The car's large LCD display showed the name "Jessica," and after connecting the call over the speaker, a female voice started asking questions about her car being shipped to Hawaii. She was apparently wondering about the date and location of its arrival.

"Let me call you back on that!" Lester said, then hung up the phone and directed his attention back to me. His voice seemed a bit nervous.

"Ready?" he asked me.

While I didn't understand what was going on with a car in Hawaii, I did realize he was talking to that college friend of his, Jessica—or Pookie, as he called her. I remembered hearing about her all too well, as Kathy liked to talk about her—a lot.

"Wait," I paused him. "Pookie now lives in Hawaii? So, she was she in Hawaii when you went there last month?"

"Yes, she was. I thought I told you about that." His voice became shaky, and his eyes had a hard time making contact with mine.

"No, Lester. You did not tell me about Pookie being there! Did you plan it that way or was it your mom's idea? She would probably rather see you with her than me anyway! Gosh darnit, I can't believe you went to Hawaii to see her after the fight we had over your trip to Houston a few years back!"

"Well, I knew you would assume the worst, so I didn't say anything. I just went because I didn't want Mom to go alone. Pookie was only there because she needed a place to stay, and Mom's friend let her move into her house."

Then he explained that they—he and Kathy—bought Jessica a car and shipped it to Hawaii. And of course, he said it had been his mom's idea to help Jessica out. The thought of Lester lying once more about his old college flame felt like a knife stabbing into my heart, twisting and turning it right in the same spot that had been injured before. I didn't even think to ask where the money came from to buy and ship a car because he didn't even have a job at the time. It didn't matter anymore. What mattered was how betrayed and double-crossed I felt. I could feel my heart breaking and shattering into a million pieces.

"Take me home," I said, tears running down my face.

"You are making a big deal out of nothing!" he said. "This was weeks ago, and nothing happened, I promise. She means nothing to me. I love you! And I'm sorry, I really thought I told you."

"Um, no. I think I would remember you saying that you'd be going to Hawaii to see your girlfriend. I want to go home. Please take me home, now!" I said quietly and in pain.

Needless to say, he kept assuring me it wasn't what it looked like. He insisted that it was all his mother's doing. She'd set him up for that, and that was why he hadn't told me. He didn't want to hurt me, and he figured it would be better not to say anything even while he was there.

As always, the way he apologized and the words he used were quite convincing. Once again, I started to feel it may have been my fault that he couldn't tell me the truth, and I definitely believed it was his mother that orchestrated the whole thing. Before it was time to go to bed, I had already forgiven him, convincing myself by thinking, *He only lied to protect me. He did not mean to hurt me.*

TRIP TO HAWAII WITH KATHY IN OCTOBER 2015 – PART 2
Then a year after he came back…

I wasn't even thinking about the trip to Hawaii anymore by the fall of 2016 until Lester and I met up at a bar. This was after we had gotten divorced, but we were still seeing each other. We got to talking about the improvement of his speech. The impediment, the stuttering and not being able to get words out correctly was still noticeable but not like the time he had lost his speech completely a few months after the trip to Hawaii. I could tell that it was a very difficult time for him because it made him feel handicapped and useless. His self-esteem had been at an all-time low, and the remaining disability continued to bother him very much as it hindered him from finding a job due to not being able to communicate properly.

"Funny to think that all of this not talking right is because I fell at the beach in Hawaii." His voice showed a bit of disappointment in himself.

I paused for a moment, gathering my memories about the trip to Hawaii. I didn't remember a fall; I only remembered that mid-trip his speech had dramatically worsened for no apparent reason.

"Wait. What? You fell? What do you mean, you fell?" I had no idea what he was talking about.

"When I fell!", he responded. "In Hawaii? That's why I lost my speech! I was fine until then, remember?" he said, looking a bit confused himself.

"What do you mean? You didn't tell me. All I know is your speech just went away from one day to another!"

I was still clueless. My good mood disappeared within seconds, and emptiness seemed to fill my heart and soul. I was scared to be told about yet another big secret that had been kept from me, afraid to be told it was for the protection of our relationship or whatever rationalization he'd come up with this time.

He said, "I really thought I told you! I was at the beach by the water, and the waves went and pulled my feet from underneath me. I fell and hit my head on the ground."

And there I was, more than a year later, finding out that his own recklessness was responsible for his speech impairment and not the accident itself. What was it with this trip to Hawaii? The pain still lingered from finding out about Pookie. Now there were more lies coming to the surface?

It all started to make sense. My thoughts started to travel back in time, remembering when it had been about midweek into the trip. He called from Hawaii, and I noticed that he had started stuttering and couldn't get some words to come out. It seemed to frustrate him. He assured me that all was well. Yet he too had noticed that something had changed. The days went by, and with each day, his ability to speak worsened. By the time he got back from Hawaii, he was no longer able to speak.

I remembered that the neurologist had concluded that things like this can, unfortunately, happen out of the blue. That is what I had believed to be the reason the whole time.

I almost want to think that his pride kept him from telling me or even the doctor the truth about the fall. So was I going to make a big deal out of this lie? Of course not. I brushed it off since it was an "old" lie, and he was now telling me what really happened. I guess this evening at the bar he had forgotten he'd chosen not to tell me the truth back then. It was more important for me to know that we were together again, aiming to leave the past in the past and work toward our future.

And yes, once again, my longing to be with him led me to find a logical reason as to why I should forgive him. I excused this lie with the reasoning that it must have been very embarrassing for him to admit that his own carelessness had caused his disability. Not only had I become numb to the pain, but I was also just happy to be with the man I loved so dearly.

We had worked hard to rekindle our love and being with him was all that mattered to me.

NOT EVEN SEIZURES WILL STOP HIM—FALL OF 2016

One evening when Lester was going to spend another night at my apartment, we were sitting on the couch watching TV, and all seemed fine. Then, from one second to another, he jumped up and just stood there with his eyes and mouth wide open. His whole body seemed to have become stiff. I didn't know what was going on, as he was shaking and turning blue.

It scared the living hell out of me. I screamed for help and yelled his name but couldn't get him to respond. I thought it was a heart attack. I called 911, and when the paramedics arrived, they determined it was a seizure. He was responsive again. Lester was going to be okay, they said. The ambulance took him to the closest hospital where he spent the night for observation. I stayed by his bedside. Memories of the accident went through my head as I watched him sleep. When he had a second episode later that night, the doctor advised him that with two seizures in a row, he was considered epileptic and would not be allowed to drive for six months as per Nevada law. That really bummed him out, but he said he understood.

We went back to the apartment at the break of dawn, and soon I had to go to work. He said he wanted to go see his mom to let her know he was okay. I assured Lester that I would take him to Kathy's home after work. I had a nagging feeling in the back of my mind that he wasn't going to wait. Before I left for work, I wrote down the mileage of his car. After work I was so excited to come home and see him feeling better that I totally forgot to check on the mileage that first evening. He also didn't ask to go to his mom's, and I was not going to remind him. But on the second day, after coming home, I was curious to see if he had left, as he didn't say anything about Kathy again. I checked the mileage, and sure enough, he had driven almost ninety miles in those two days. Of course, I wasn't sure where else he'd gone, but I was sure he'd gone to his mom's. I decided to ask him whether he'd driven to find out if he would continue this masquerade. He was lying down in the recliner looking quite comfortable when I approached him about it.

"Hey babes, how are you feeling? How was your day? Did you miss me?" I leaned forward and kissed him on the forehead.

He said, "Boring but okay. Just sitting here waiting for you to come home."

"You were home all day?" I asked as if I didn't know of his excursion.

He said, "Yes, of course! I am not allowed to drive, remember?"

I asked again to give him a chance to reconsider. He lied again. When I confronted him about the mileage, he first got mad about the fact that I didn't trust him. He then admitted that he had gone to see Kathy both days. He just wanted to make sure she was okay and not worried about him. *Shouldn't it be the other way around?* I wondered. I couldn't believe that he had driven right after having two major seizures. Could not even that keep him from seeing his mother? Here I was, all worried about his health, and once again, he felt comfortable having secrets from me for two days straight.

All I could think of was the fact he could have had another seizure while driving, causing another accident, maybe even hurting or killing someone else. And what was even worse was the realization that his lies didn't seem to end. I was so disappointed. Not just in him but also in myself for allowing Lester to keep playing the same card over and over again to convince me of his innocence.

"I knew you didn't want me to, so I didn't want to tell you—so you wouldn't get mad!" was his response when I asked why he had lied to me again.

I told him that I was done and that he needed to pack his belongings and go home to his mom. I offered him a ride, but he declined. After that, I thought I was finally done. I was mad, hurt, and quite disappointed—mostly in myself for letting him do me like that.

After a few months, I made it known that I was officially divorced. After I mentioned on social media that I had gone on a few dinner dates, he wrote me a letter that made my heart melt. It seemed like he realized he had gone too far this time and he was terribly sorry. It was the way he wrote it that got me, capturing all our incredibly special moments from the past. I was impressed by how well he remembered all the details he described in his letter. I just couldn't resist the man I loved so dearly. So yes, I gave in once again, convinced he spoke with sincerity about this being his last lie.

We started dating again, and by early 2017, he got down on one knee and presented a beautiful big diamond ring while asking me to marry him once more. I was so happy. For almost two years after the accident, I had tried to get my husband's love and devotion back, and finally he seemed to put me before his mom. I found out he had even started going to church on his own and had joined a men's prayer group. I really believed that this was a new beginning and that things would be different this time.

RESEARCH
Per the Merriam-Webster 2021 online edition

a *lie*

1a. an assertion of something known or believed by the speaker or writer to be untrue with intent to deceive

Example sentence: He told a *lie* to avoid punishment.

1b. an untrue or inaccurate statement that may or may not be believed true by the speaker or writer

Example sentences: The *lies* we tell ourselves to feel better...

2. something that misleads or deceives

Example sentence: His show of remorse was a *lie*.

In my research, I found in an online article from *Psychology Today* magazine that explains that the most obvious trait of a narcissist is not only the lies but lies with a different motive behind them. The fact that people hide the truth in and of itself is nothing extraordinary, as it is a trait of every human being. *"It's estimated that most of us lie almost every day,"* says the article. The difference is that the narcissist's lies or efforts to hide the truth are central to the narcissist's identity. *"Of course, he doesn't see it that way because all his experiences are filtered through the hidden damage; instead, he will see it as his truth."*

The same article explains that due to their lack of empathy, the narcissist will lie without blinking an eye. If they are certain that their version of truth promotes what is in their best interest, that makes it okay for them to lie.

The article further says that it appears that even children know the difference between truth and lies. Children know that telling the truth is the right thing to do and that telling a lie is wrong and will have consequences. For the narcissist, lies are justified to protect whatever is necessary to ensure an ideal outcome. Once caught in a lie, they will often defer the blame to the accuser.

This matches the reasons that Lester would use to excuse his untruthfulness:

"I knew you wouldn't like to hear the truth, and I didn't want you to be upset" or…

"I had to do something! If I had told you the truth, you would have gotten angry like you are now" or…

"If you had asked me, I would have told you, but you didn't ask!"

With Lester, his lies were constant. I honestly cannot give you a clear number of how many times I was lied to, as I came to realize that anything he ever told me could have been a lie. For example, Lester's convincing story that he had worked for a TV show as an audio installer could be true, or it could be a lie. He did have a lot of Hollywood insider knowledge, as he watched a great amount of TV, but maybe it was just an added fantasy detail to sound more convincing in his claim of being a high-paid audio installer. There was no real rhyme or reason for his lies other than to present himself as respectable or to avoid facing the consequences of a challenging situation. Any number of things I'd been told by him could be a complete fantasy for all I know.

TAKEAWAY

I realize that I had become numb to Lester's lies. I did not see that at the time though. I also now think that he didn't even feel bad when he was fabricating his version of the truth. It seems keeping secrets or telling lies was his way of keeping things calm and in order regardless of the cost. And in my hopes of better days, I convinced myself every time that I was seeing signs of positive changes in his behavior.

I had trained myself to believe that when he lied to me, it was not to intentionally hide anything from me but rather because that's all he knew to do. This explanation was good enough for me and excused each and every lie he would tell. "I didn't know how you would react" or "I knew you wouldn't like the truth" were his most prevalent reasons. And I, befuddled and so in love with my otherwise perfect husband, saw myself as the patient and understanding wife that surely would change her husband at some point and convince him to drop his dishonesty.

Looking back, I realize that all the compounded lies destroyed my ability to trust my husband. The process of destruction went so slowly and so quietly that I didn't even notice. I had become dense to the fact that lies do not belong in a good relationship regardless of whether it's a friendship, a partnership, or a marriage. Lies destroy trust. I still hear myself excuse him with "Other than the lies, he is the kindest man with the biggest heart, and he treats me like a queen!" which led me to excuse every dishonesty with the reason "That's because of the way he was raised. He doesn't mean to hurt me; he just doesn't know any better." I would either find blame in the mother or in myself for being too controlling, possessive, or distrusting.

It didn't come to me until much later that regardless of how a person was raised, there comes a point when they're old enough to make decisions for themselves. And just because a person was raised a certain way does not give them permission to behave in a morally wrong way, even if it is the only way they've known.

Lies are unacceptable and should never be ignored the way I ignored them.

MOVING FORWARD

CAN A NARCISSIST CHANGE FOR THE BETTER?

It is possible, but only if they are well aware of their wrongdoing and willing to go through the courageous process of self-discovery. Then again, this in itself sounds quite contradictory to me. We *are* talking about narcissists: people who, by nature, have little heed for conscience and self-discovery of wrongdoing. For them to change, they would have to go against their very nature.

But how do you know your partner is lying? Ask yourself these questions:

- ☑ Is there anything that doesn't seem to add up? *Feel free to use common sense and your gut feelings.*

- ☑ Do they go missing for any amount of time—short or long? *Letting each other know where you are is part of trust, not a matter of control. You should not be in the dark about their whereabouts.*

- ☑ Do they show signs of deceit in their body language (*e.g., avoid eye contact, point their body away from you, overall act strange or nervous, face their palms downward when they talk to you, exhibit unusual fidgeting or foot-tapping*)?

- ☑ Do they have a hard time giving you a straight answer when you ask them questions (*e.g., mumbling answers, questioning your concern, repeating your question in their answer, being vague and defensive, or avoiding a discussion*)?

Keep in mind that your answers are not proof that they are or are not a liar, but these questions can help you evaluate your situation, nonetheless.

If you experience a persistent liar in your life who is not willing to change, you could choose to accept that they habitually lie, ruling out trust in your relationship. Anything they say could be a lie or half-truth. They may withhold information from you as they see fit. But for obvious reasons, I don't recommend it. Lies are lies, and they do not belong in any relationship.

In my own experience, I suggest standing up for yourself, your morals, and your ethics. Walk away if you cannot trust your partner.

Understand that no matter how kind and loving and loyal and truthful you are, you cannot teach a narcissist to become an honest person. It is not in their nature, and it is not your job or responsibility to even begin to try to fix them. Any attempt to convince them will be a dead end, and you will be the one getting hurt in the process. There will come a point when you either give up or give out, meaning you will run out of strength to move forward.

If you catch yourself thinking, *Those lies? They don't count*: stop! You would be lying to yourself, and that's that.

In the next chapter, you will hear the rest of the story about Lester and me. If you thought we were done with the emotional roller coaster, you are in for another ride. "Wash, Rinse, Repeat" is the title of the chapter, and it's designed without lecturing to let you pick out some hidden red flags based on the research you've heard so far. It should serve quite well as a little practice session for you.

CHAPTER 7

WASH, RINSE, REPEAT

BACKGROUND STORY

MOVING IN TOGETHER—THE THREE OF US

Being engaged to Lester for the second time felt like such a relief. Somehow, I imagined that everything would be different from here on out—no more secrets, complete honesty, and devotion to each other. Sounded simple enough to me.

"Where will we live?" he asked me, realizing that we would move in together once again.

Considering our financial situation, I assured him that it would be fine for us to live in his house with his mom. I explained that she would have to step aside, that we would pack up all her belongings and make the house ours as a couple. He agreed, as nothing in his house made him feel like it was his home. While he had paid for everything, it was all set up by Kathy, so he had no emotional ties to any of it. He actually seemed excited to change the interior to make it *our* home instead of hers.

In mid-April of 2018, I moved in. We boxed up all her belongings and moved in our old furniture mixed with some of the existing pieces. In order to set boundaries, we explained to Kathy that she would no longer use Lester's master bathroom but would use her own: the full bath right off the hallway. I decided I would do our laundry, as I didn't want her to have any part of that anymore. I mentioned she could do her own, or I could do it for her. Things like cooking and cleaning would be shared as we went along.

After a few days, I noticed that something was very wrong. Lester had told me her behavior had changed after a surgery she underwent to remove a cancerous spot on the side of her face. She had started doing extremely weird things like wrapping random items into layers of plastic bags, putting food in her nightstand, or losing track of what she was doing. Now with me there, she would get terribly angry at me for no reason, use cuss words I'd never heard her use before, and be more hateful than ever. I started to have some doubts as to whether the living arrangement was really going to work.

KATHY GETS VIOLENT

One day, Lester came home from his new job with a local audio installation business, having picked up his trade from many years ago. He put his cash earnings—a small stack of twenty-dollar bills from his new job—on the counter and went into the back to take his bath. Then I came home from work as well and placed my car keys on top of the bills, as I didn't want to scratch up the surface of the wood with them. Kathy was so anal about keeping everything like new that I only meant well by doing so.

Kathy saw this and started getting in my face yelling, "Don't touch my son's money! That is not your money! You don't put your key on this money! That's for me, not you!"

I told her that she was wrong about that, and before I knew it, she had her brittle hands around my throat, choking me as hard as she could. While it scared me, she was not strong enough to actually do any major harm, so I removed both of her hands from my neck and said, "Kathy, don't you ever do that again." When I told Lester what had happened later that evening, he apologized but didn't know what else to say. He did agree that something had to be done.

Before we could even talk about that some more, Kathy had another violent outburst — and this one didn't end as easily. I was doing laundry when she approached me in the little utility room, holding Lester's underwear in my face. She told me it wasn't mine, it was *her* son's, and just a moment later, she started throwing her little fists in my face. To defend myself, I raised my arm and accidentally knocked her glasses into her nose. She had very thin skin, so the impact of the glasses on her nose caused the brittle skin to break. I could see little droplets of blood trying to escape the small cut.

I pushed her away, not violently but firmly. I didn't want to hurt her. I just needed her to back away. She disappeared quickly, and I called Lester to tell him what had happened. While I was on the phone, I began to hear commotion on the street. There she was in the neighbor's driveway, both arms scratched up with blood running down to drip off her hands. I knew I hadn't done all that, so I asked what she had done. That's when the neighbor told me to stay away from

Kathy. Apparently, she'd told him I had beaten her up, so he had called the police. I had a feeling she scratched her arms herself to cause them to bleed so she could claim that I harmed her. Lester rushed home in the meantime.

GOING TO JAIL

When the police came, they evaluated the situation. While I had a bloodshot eye from Kathy's fists hitting me, she was standing there with her arms scratched open. It was explained to me that in the state of Nevada, a person was guaranteed to go to jail after a violent domestic disturbance like this. And just from the matter of the age difference and physical build, I was charged with battery, handcuffed, and transported to the downtown city jail.

I felt so out of place while in detention. It was humiliating and disgusting. I spent the whole time in a small holding cell together with prostitutes, drug addicts, and criminals. I listened to trashy talk, comparisons of who had been in jail the most, and ate food that made me gag with every bite. The room offered bare concrete benches all along the walls to sleep on. I froze terribly in the well air-conditioned facility, as I only had a T-shirt and shorts on and was not allowed to grab a jacket during the arrest. There was one metal toilet and a tiny metal sink in one corner. If you wanted to use the bathroom, it was in view of all the others in the cell. I was scared but trusted God to take care of me. I had never had anything to do with the law. The worst I had on my record was a few speeding tickets from some years back. Now I found myself charged with domestic violence and assault.

Lester finally bailed me out on the third day. I felt nasty; I had not showered or brushed my hair or teeth the whole time. After this event, we did not waste another moment and decided to seal our love right then and there. Coming straight out of the jail building, we went to the courthouse a few blocks away and got our marriage license. Then we rode in a courtesy limousine that took us to a nearby wedding chapel and got married. To us, it was just a matter of straightening out in documentation what was wrongly done a couple of years back. The date was April 30, 2017.

From then on, Kathy stayed in her room most of the time when I was home. Her crazy moods and actions continued and gradually got worse. It went from bad to unpredictable and crazy, until one day we came home from work and the whole house was flooded. She had clogged up the toilet with paper and had tried to fix it. While fumbling inside the water tank, the water supply mechanism got stuck and the tank overflowed for four hours straight.

"We need to get her checked; I think she has Alzheimer's!" I told him.

"That would explain her moods and why she hasn't kept up with the bills," he responded.

DIAGNOSIS—ALZHEIMER'S

After a few visits to the local specialist, my theory was confirmed, and Kathy was diagnosed with Alzheimer's disease. No wonder Kathy hadn't kept up with the bills. Knowing that Lester relied on his mother regarding all financial affairs, I checked on the finances. The mortgage and a few other bills were seven months behind, the house was under foreclosure, and we were about to be put out on the street. Lester admitted he'd known but didn't have any answers as to how to fix the situation. He agreed it would be best to provide me with the power of attorney for him and his mom to take care of everything that needed to be done. I got several loans between him and me and was able to pay back all those that were behind. Now we had had new loans to pay off on top of the existing ones, including the thousands of dollars owed to the IRS for gambling winnings. I felt overwhelmed.

In August, Kathy had some severe digestive issues that led us to take her to the emergency room. After being treated for a few days, they were ready to release her. We talked to the doctors and explained that there was no way we could take her home, as she wouldn't be safe by herself while we had to be at work. They transferred her over to a rehabilitation center that she seemed to like quite well. She was still unpredictable in her moods during our visits. I tried not to go near her, as she would just get angry when I did.

Even though the living arrangement was all straightened out, I was informed that we were facing more upcoming challenges. The crimes Kathy and Lester had committed by delivering drugs up until to the day he had the accident had finally caught up with them. It was not the accident that brought it to light. Lester told me that someone must have contacted the FBI who then had stormed his and his mom's house in March of 2016, just a few months after our divorce. At that time, the Bureau found $140,000 stashed away and the ledger that Kathy kept in her obsession to document everything, including all income and expenses from their trips to California, which gave the FBI plenty of evidence to press heavy charges.

Kathy's detailed bookkeeping made it easy for the FBI to charge both, her and Lester alike, with possession with intent to distribute and a few other things. The overall number that legal documents from court hearings in New York showed was that over the years, Lester and his mom had delivered drugs worth over 1.4 million dollars. There were a few court hearings in Syracuse, New York, before Lester was sentenced in December to four years of prison camp. He was ordered to surrender on January 9, 2018, to the low-security portion of the only federal supermax penitentiary in the United States in Florence, Colorado.

Kathy had the same charges filed against her by the FBI. It took me a good amount of paperwork and doctor visits to get the criminal case filed against her dropped. Otherwise, she would have ended up in prison too.

ALL ALONE IN THAT BIG HOUSE

There I was. This is not what I'd had in mind when I remarried my husband. But with everything that we had been through, I was so very sure this was the last hurdle we'd have to overcome: this together-apartness thing.

A few weeks after he left, I had my own domestic battery court date about the incident with Kathy to deal with. I was able to get it dismissed, but it had become part of my permanent record. It wouldn't show on background checks for job applications, but I was told it would be visible to anything court or police related.

Just a few months after Lester left, I had the opportunity to switch jobs from one customer service company to another. I now worked from home with better pay and lots of opportunities to work overtime. With all the unpaid bills and loans taken out to get caught up, I took any chance I could to earn extra income. I remember working close to eighty hours a week during peak seasons. Working this much kept my mind busy too. Lester wrote quick emails here and there and was able to call every three to four days.

I was able to go visit him every three to four months. It was a fifteen-hour drive each way, partially through the beautiful mountains of Colorado. We would visit for five to six hours on Saturday as well as Sunday before I would take the long trip to get home, just in time to clock in again. I worked hard to keep our budget on track. I didn't spend any money except for what was necessary and managed to pay off most of his debt and our household bills. I also sent him money every month. He told me it was for razors and haircuts. Everything in prison was overpriced or hard to get.

Within a year, I had Kathy moved from the regular care center into a closed institution for dementia. One reason was that she was officially diagnosed with late-stage Alzheimer's in the past year. The disease was progressing quite fast, and it required specially trained nurses to take care of her.

Another reason was that one of Lester's friends, William, who had often borrowed money from Kathy in the old days, had made his way into Kathy's life in the nursing home. He managed to replace my name as her main contact with his and his wife's. He even replaced Lester's photos in her room with his and started buying her cute little teddy bears that said "I love you" on them. He then changed Kathy's mailing address from our house to his, basically receiving all her bank statements and other sensitive information. When I asked Lester about this on one of our calls, he said that he had asked William to keep an eye on Kathy since he didn't expect me to do so after everything that she had put me through. However, he did not tell him to change the address to be forwarded to him.

I believed him—as I tended to do all those years—and changed the mail back and filed a complaint for extortion of the elderly at the police station against William. There was nothing I could do other than change her address back and make sure William was not allowed to see her in the new facility. I never did like him much and had reason to mistrust him. In the past, he'd visit Kathy for years even when Lester was not home, and she would provide him with a few hundred dollars here and there that Lester didn't know of until sometime later. I assumed he hoped to maybe get something out of her, while Lester claimed it was all a misunderstanding. I never did find out the truth about this.

KATHY GETS WORSE

With Kathy's memory depleting more and more, she stopped recognizing me, and with that, stopped being hateful toward me. However, the nurses told me she wouldn't hesitate to start a fight with the other residents. Every few weeks, I would get a courtesy call to notify me that she had hit someone or that another patient had scratched her in self-defense. With her not knowing who I was anymore, I would visit her about once a month and show her pictures on my phone of my kids and her son. She would start crying most of the time, wishing he would come home. Her English was never the best, but now it started to disappear more and more. She would say a few words in English but then switch back over to Hungarian. I would pretend I understood, as I simply wanted to make sure she was okay so I could update Lester on our next phone call.

The more time that went by, the more I had the opportunity to work on forgiving her for everything she had put me through. My weekly visits to church helped me to understand that forgiveness was not meant to excuse her hateful actions against me in the past nor judge what was right or wrong in any situation. Forgiveness was to soften my heart, to remove the scars, and to allow me to love her as my sister in Christ. It was a long, bumpy road—this road to forgiveness. I had to fight inner battles to overcome the anger I had stored up inside me over the years. I must admit it was one of the hardest spiritual challenges I've ever experienced, but it was also the most rewarding one. I think this is why my church once had us do an exercise where we put the name of someone we had to forgive on a rock and place it at the bottom of the cross that they had set up in the large entrance hall of the church. Once you experience the true feeling of forgiveness for just one person, the peace it brings with it makes it so much easier—almost instinctive and natural—to forgive others.

By the beginning of 2020, Kathy was like a ghost wandering the hallways; she was down to only ninety five pounds and hardly spoke anymore. She would still cry when she saw

Lester's photo and point to him. I believe she still recognized him, as he was the one that she had spent every day of the last thirty years with. She would not react to the photos where he was wearing a beard though, just those without facial hair. By then, I had also made complete peace with all the things she had done to me. I felt a need—almost a responsibility as a Christian—to guide her to find God.

While she had been a Catholic for all her life and had read the Bible, she held a grudge against God for almost forty years for taking her husband away from her. I truly felt it was then—when she was at a painful stage in her life, grieving for her husband—that she was influenced by evil, convincing her to keep her grudges and to be hateful toward others. At least that is how I explained it to myself, and it helped my healing process. I learned that the Devil does not ask for acceptance. He'll speak in disguise with the voice of God, convincing a person to follow ways that are harmful, hurtful, or just plain evil, while letting that person believe it's for good. The Devil takes advantage of moments in a person's life when they find themselves vulnerable and desperately looking for love or affection.

Now I know this doesn't excuse the behavior. It simply explains what happened. That person still has free will and is able to make decisions. I believe the poor conditions that Kathy grew up in and the wish as an immigrant for a better life in the US drove her to choose the "wrong voice" to listen to and believe. And with that, I truly believe her actions were evil, driven by the Devil for all these years that she was healthy and of a clear mind. Then though, as the Alzheimer's disease progressed, the Kathy that I had known to hate me and the world around her started to become nicer to me with every visit at the nursing home. It seemed to me as her days on Earth came to an end, the devil had no longer the power to manipulate the now mindless body. It was as if he had finally released Kathy.

All that was left was a shell, yet a child of God, and it was my job to ensure that her journey would lead her to her creator. I did everything I could think of to fulfill this goal. In her last few weeks, we prayed together almost daily. I would read from the Bible, talk to her, and read her Christian stories of love and togetherness. I wanted to honor the fact that she was Catholic and called a priest to provide her with the last rites. It was just a few days later on March 14, 2020, that she took her last breath. The nursing home called me the morning after my last visit with her to let me know she had passed.

I am sure Lester had his own personal moments to actually grieve, but he seemed to take it rather well when I told him on the phone. I had kept him updated on her progress, and he thanked me for being there for her when he couldn't. He told me that he never thought he would not get to see her again when he'd left two years ago.

After making sure that it was in her will, I had her cremated and set up a little memorial for her in the front window of our entrance. Her urn, her photo, her rosary, and her Bible were nicely displayed and decorated with some black lace and flowers. Since Lester didn't get to be there, I wanted to do what I felt was honorable for his mother.

LESTER COMES HOME FROM PRISON EARLY

In the meantime, the virus COVID-19 had fully developed, so I did research as to what it would take to get Lester out of prison early due to his health conditions and the CDC regulations in place. He still had over a year of imprisonment ahead of him. After thorough investigation, I formulated a letter to the Federal Bureau of Prisons that apparently had enough impact for him to be sent home on house arrest. He was going to be the first one to be released from that particular prison on a so-called medical furlough. He seemed more eager than thankful to get out, as he'd never really seen a reason for him to be behind bars in the first place. In his eyes, he was falsely imprisoned and never did see himself as a criminal.

Since his conviction, he stated many times that he should be entitled to receive the $140,000 that was found by the FBI in the house. He claimed these were gambling winnings, to the point where he had written a few times to the church's men's group that he had joined to gather $5,000 in a GoFundMe collection so he could hire an attorney to get this money back. I was upset at him for doing that. He'd committed a crime and deserved to be behind bars. I asked him to look at the beautiful things in life instead. Unlike most prisoners, he had a loyal and hardworking wife at home and was able to look forward to a home, a car, and a wonderful future. None of that really lifted his spirits, it seemed. He stuck with his opinion that he had been done wrong by the judgment against him.

A total of two years and five months—what seemed like an eternity to me—had gone by before his early release from prison. He was ordered to wear an ankle bracelet and was only allowed to leave the house on approved occasions like going to work or weekly shopping at the grocery store. When he first came home, he appeared thankful to be out, but things quickly took a turn in his attitude toward his newly gained freedom. We had talked many times about how tight I had to keep the budget for all those years to survive. If I did have a few extra dollars, they went toward outstanding debt. I saved money by eating the bare minimum with hardly any treats.

But when he came home, it seemed that all his talk about how anything would be better than prison food was forgotten. For example, when I asked out of courtesy if there was anything he wanted me to get from the store, he asked for sparkling water. And he didn't want the cheap kind; he asked for it to be Perrier. Granted, that wouldn't be a major issue, except that he knew I'd been drinking faucet water all this time, and it upset me that the same wasn't good enough for him.

Weeks went by, and he spent his days mostly watching TV. In conversations with other ex-prisoners' wives, I was told it may take some time for him to adjust, so I tried to be understanding and didn't rush him to find a job. I did try to nudge him to start looking, though, as our funds were running low.

ONE. LAST. LIE.

Only a month after his release, I decided to go on a short weekend trip to see one of my kids now that I finally had the chance. When I got back, all seemed fine until he bent over to give me a kiss right after my return. I smelled smoke on his breath. I couldn't believe it. He didn't smoke for over two years, and his desire to smoke was stronger than my request for him to never pick up a cigarette again? Or maybe he did smoke in prison? Maybe that would explain the constant requests for money to buy new razors? But that was not what got me. It was the lie that followed.

"Did you smoke?" I asked him.

"Me? No!" he said as if I was accusing him of something very unreasonable.

Supposedly he didn't smoke in prison; it wasn't allowed. Today I am not sure if this was true or not, but he said everyone else would smoke and he would not. And yes, of course, I believed him. We had talked in the past about how I would quit as well and that we wouldn't pick the habit back up when he got out. He snored badly and smoking didn't help that, nor did it help his overall health.

"Your breath when you kissed me, I smelled it. So let me ask you again, Lester. Did you smoke?"

"Just one, I borrowed one while I was out shopping earlier."

Mind you, when we first met, he pretended for several months that he didn't smoke by carefully using gum and washing his hands. He'd mastered disguising it until I smelled it one day. Since I used to be a smoker myself sometime before I met him, his smoking led me to start up again. While he was in prison, I had quit again and was looking forward to a smoke-free life once he got out.

"Just one? Really?" I continued my questioning, "You mean to tell me I was gone for three days, and you wait until I am almost home to have one smoke?"

"Well, maybe I had like five or so while you were gone." he replied.

I had also sworn to myself that if Lester were to lie just *once* after getting out of prison, I would leave him in an instant. I didn't care if it was a little lie or a big lie. I'd decided I was not going to tolerate lies any longer. I truly hoped that the time in prison would show him how much he had waiting for him at home. I thought he would come out with an appreciation for everything he still had.

"So now you tell me you bummed five cigarettes? I think you bought a pack as soon as I left!"

He finally came out and said yes, he had bought a pack. It took me a few moments to think and let it sink in. I had a decision to make. Which one was stronger, my promise to myself to no longer accept his lies or my love for him?

He lied to me. Nothing big. Just a little lie, I heard myself thinking.

I also thought about everything I had learned about narcissists and their lies. For two years, I had told myself to stand my ground—that if he came home and lied *one* more time I would walk away.

Was this my sign? Was this the "walk away" signal—a stupid lie like this? I was trying to find excuses as to why I should not have pushed him to lie. I blamed myself for a few moments, told myself it was my fault, that I shouldn't have been so selfish as to tell him not to smoke. Then I reminded myself that it wasn't about smoking at all. It was about the fact that he was still hiding things from me then lying to me about it. Lastly, it was about the promise I had made to myself!

I had to find my focus. *Remember your promise to yourself. Walk away if he lies, remember?* I kept hearing this over and over in my head...

It was then at that moment that I realized even after over two years in prison, two years of dedicating my life to waiting for him, he'd just crushed all my hopes and dreams. The trust I had built back up was gone in an instant, and all it took was one little lie.

"I am so done, Lester! I am done with your lies. I can't do this anymore. Your mom ain't the reason no more, she is gone! I worked so hard, and you still don't think I deserve honesty from you?" I started crying. I felt so torn between my love for him and the promise to myself.

"I'll let you know what I'm gonna do, but I am done chasing after you, getting lied at, getting betrayed over stupid stuff," I continued.

He looked at me with that look that gave me the feeling I'd said something I shouldn't have, or I'd said something wrong.

My mind was rushing, and I caught thoughts of doubt. *Eight years with this man, two and a half working hard and waiting just for him to come home, and just a month later I want to throw it all away? Just like that?* I redirected my thoughts to reality. *He lied. It's all just a wash, rinse, repeat. This is never going to stop. If two years didn't stop the lies, nothing will.* I went into the bathroom to clear my head for a moment. This was a moment I was not prepared for. But I was done with the lies—finally. I washed my face before going back into the living room.

"I believe that you have much to work through and sort out now that you are back. We both do. But you will need to find yourself and figure out what you want most in your life. How can I trust you if you lie over something like smoking?"

"All this because I smoked? Smoking to me represents my freedom! It's the only thing in my life that I feel like I have control over, and you want to take that away from me! Are you serious?" he asked.

"Lester, you've got it all so wrong if you think you have control over smoking. Don't you get it? It's the other way around! Smoking controls you. With how this is going, I don't even know if you really did quit in prison or if you smoked the whole time you were there. But who cares? The smoking doesn't matter. I don't care anymore. It's not the point. It's the lying I can't handle."

CLOSING TIME

Weeks went by with little conversation. Lester finally found a job, once again as audio installer. He took out a loan and bought a car. He knew he had to find a place to live very soon but didn't put in much effort to find a place. The house sold rather quickly, and I arranged all that was necessary for me to move to North Carolina. Just a month later, I was all moved out. He moved in with an old friend in town. Everything was divided quickly and fairly, as I didn't seek any gain from any of this. I just wanted to get as far away as possible, as I knew quite well that if I stuck around, I would want to see him, and my heart would just melt as it did every time when we separated. I still loved him. I still loved the kind man who I believed I married eight years ago. But the moment he lied about smoking was the moment I finally woke up. Everything I invested into earning his love and devotion over the years was nothing but a waste. Like a vase that had been broken so many times and glued back together, eventually, there comes a time it can no longer be repaired.

I felt like he needed time away from me to discover who *he* really was without having to please his mother and without me to rely on to fix every challenge life presents. I also thought it would help him learn to take full responsibility for earning an honest income, while getting accustomed to living on a budget that he alone controlled. We agreed to wait a year before making a final decision about us, giving both of us some time to think. Living separately would do us good. There was no need to rush into another divorce. At this point, I still didn't want to lose him. I didn't want to go on as it was, but against all common sense, I was still not ready to give up. We still talked every couple of days after my move. Our conversations still ended with the familiar "I love you."

OUR LAST PHONE CONVERSATION—OCTOBER 2020
Then one night he asked about the money and the proceeds from the house. I told him I used it to pay our bills. I let him know that we'd both ended up with about the same amount of debt.

"There's nothing left? What do you mean there is nothing left? You told me I get twenty-five hundred dollars! What happened to that?" his voice went from nice to angry within moments.

"That was when you said you needed it to get your own place! We added it up because you said you needed first rent, last rent, and a deposit. But then you moved in with your friend you said. Come to find out that was lie because you actually moved in with that William guy and you didn't want me to know! With that, you didn't have those moving costs, and I used that money toward more of our bills. What did you think? You get to walk away with cash in your pocket? I didn't get pocket money, what makes you think you would?"

"I can't believe you spent all the money from *my* house, and I didn't even get what you told me I would! Well, that's it then!" he hung up. He immediately blocked me from almost all communication and social media. I was able to email him, but there were no responses.

Once again, I was left in the dark, heartbroken and confused.

Did he not tell me the night before that he loved me? But tonight, after he asks for cash and hears there isn't any, we're done? Was he only keeping in touch in order to follow up and see if there was any cash left? How many times can I be crushed? How can I be so blind to think he still loves me?

I wasn't even hurting anymore. I had nothing left in me to be hurting. Sure, I had my moments when I cried. I was missing the soulmate I once thought I had found. I spent eight years of my life fighting for a man who existed only in my dreams.

How many times will it take for me to understand that all the hopes I've placed in this man who I love so dearly were useless? How many times can I go through waking up to the same realization but then falling for the same spiel over and over, hoping he's changed, hoping he loves me, hoping he's true.

Instead of curling up in a ball and crying myself to sleep, I had to stay strong. I wasn't quite sure what God had in mind for my next chapter in life, but I did know I would consider everything that had happened in the last eight years. I would take what I'd learned, accomplished, and gained from them and put it to use. I wouldn't see it as a waste but rather as an opportunity for emotional, spiritual, and even intellectual growth.

A few weeks later, I was served with divorce papers—once again. He was asking for alimony and claimed that I had committed marital waste. He demanded $30,000 from me, which was the profit made on the house. In a few virtual mediation meetings, I showed evidence that all the money was used to pay our joint bills. He didn't care. He wanted "his" money.

The virtual hearings kept getting postponed. He continued to demand money, disregarding the work I had put in while he was in prison. Even after I showed proof that all debt and assets were already equally divided, it did not matter to him that I had provided a clean slate for both of us.

In the end, I realized it truly was all about the money for him.

———————————

During revision—the final process of writing this book—Lester passed away unexpectedly on April 22, 2021.

Just two days prior to his death, he sent me a text where he wrote: "I am withdrawing my petition."

The cause of death was a heart attack because of the combination of high blood pressure, obesity, coronary heart disease, and smoking. In my eyes, this list should also include "consequences from life-long anxiety, depression, and emotional distress due to mother-enmeshment." I truly believe that the root of all these issues is the silent abuse he received in his younger years, and like a snowball effect, the issues became bigger and bigger until Lester's body was not able to take it anymore.

May you finally rest in peace, my Love.

—YOUR FOREVER WIFEY, MICHA

———————————

By the way: I was right about not trusting William (now his roommate) for all these years. After Lester's death, he refused contact with me, kept thousands of dollars' worth of Lester's belongings, including the remains and belongings of Kathy, and our little six-year-old dog Keno that we got right after our first wedding. I didn't go after any of it, as I was tired and emotionally drained from taking care of other important matters that I was left with as a widow.

CHAPTER 8

MARRIED TO MOM

BACKGROUND STORY

I realized after everything that happened, after all my googling and researching, that Kathy was just another human being who had hurt and pains that led her to behave, act, and react the way she did. There was a good chance she herself had been a victim of some sort of narcissism, emotional abuse, or enmeshment. *Psychology Today* says that narcissism usually gets passed down from one generation to the next.

You may find yourself in the middle of turmoil with a narcissistic mother-in-law. What is it that you can do? What is it that you shouldn't? How deep is the mother's narcissism embedded into your husband's personality? Is there hope? How do you deal with your spouse's parent?

This chapter will hopefully answer a lot of your questions.

First, let me introduce you to my mother-in-law and our relationship a little bit more in depth. It was her behavior after all that shaped and formed Lester's character and consequently influenced his ability—or inability—to be in a healthy relationship throughout adulthood.

———————————

KATHY

Kathy was born in 1938 in Hungary where she later met her husband. In the early '70s, they defected out of the communist country via Italy and moved to the United States with the American dream many immigrants had back then. They longed for freedom, success, and financial stability. Their first and only son, Lester Alexander, was born in 1974 in the suburbs of Los Angeles, named after his father whose name was also Lester. Photos of the past showed a humble home; the father worked at the local newspaper while Kathy would do odds jobs like housekeeping and laundry services to help with the bills.

Lester was not the first child, though. According to one of my many conversations with Lester about his mom, she had been pregnant with a child about a year before his birth. When she found out it was going to be a girl, she aborted the baby with the reason that she was only going to have one child and it had to be a boy. I am sure this decision had a great impact on how she raised Lester, considering the sacrifice against her own religion as a Catholic to then bring Lester into this world. I am unsure to what level she held this over his head, but the fact alone that she told him indicates to me early signs of emotional manipulation.

When young Lester reached school age, Kathy enrolled him in the nearby Catholic school where he served as an altar boy for the attached church. In 1983, Kathy lost her husband suddenly due to heart failure when her son was only nine years of age. The year after her husband's death, she showed extreme signs of depression and was prescribed medication to help normalize her daily behavior. It appears that this was the time when things started to shift in her behavior toward her son.

Especially after her husband's passing, she became very attached to Lester. Without a doubt, she loved him. But she did not love her son like any other mom would. She seemed rather obsessed with him. She kept every card she ever wrote him for his birthday or any other holiday, as well as the cards that he wrote her, of course. She had them nicely and neatly gathered with school drawings, achievements, a letter from the Catholic priest that taught Lester in school, and photos that showed Kathy with him, and sometimes with Lester's father. She kept these memorabilia like a shrine inside a bookshelf over all those years until we moved her into the nursing home.

By the time Lester went to college, she had managed to sell the original home that her late husband had bought, and she had purchased a different one. She spent a lot of money to get it renovated from top to bottom to the point that Lester felt the need to quit college to take on a job to support his mother's spending. A decade later, they sold the home to move to Las Vegas. Lester, now in his early thirties, remained a bachelor and stuck by her side for all this time.

KATHY AND ME

There was excitement and secrecy in Lester's voice when we talked about our first Valentine's Day together just a couple of weeks after we met. He was giggly and almost exuberant about something. I could not quite figure it out but had a hunch that he had some big surprise planned for me. My curiosity had grown, and I was so excited for this special day to come. It was a few days prior to this that his mother pulled me aside.

We were alone in the kitchen, and she said in her Hungarian accent, "Micha, Lester has come to me, and we talked about it, and it is supposed to be a surprise, but he has something very special for you for Valentine's. He is going to Los Angeles this weekend to pick up a car for you."

"A car?" I asked with my eyes wide open in disbelief.

She said, "Yes, but don't tell him I told you."

Then she handed me a pair of used driving gloves and said, "Here, this is a gift from me to you. You now will have a classy car, and these will make you a classy woman."

I wasn't sure what to say, so I just said, "Thank you," unsure whether to be grateful or dumbfounded.

I was also in shock. Much since it was a car, but more as *to* why she would spoil his surprise? She knew that he wanted to surprise me! Her eyes spoke of satisfaction. Why would she do something like that? And what is the deal with these gloves? Nobody wears driving gloves. *This ain't Hollywood* were the words that went through my head.

In my naïve thinking, I thought maybe she thought telling me this secret would help us to bond. I had no plausible explanation as to why she would ruin his surprise.

Now I was stuck, pretty much forced to lie to him and to act like I knew nothing about the car, which of course would make me feel guilty. Or I could spoil the moment and tell him about his mother destroying the surprise. Was that her intent? I chose to go against my morals of being honest, which constructed my first deceit toward the man I was falling in love with. I betrayed him over a promise to his mother not to tell.

While it seemed simply inappropriate or weird at that moment, I can now clearly see all three of the main traits of narcissism in this little example with the gloves. Grandiosity, attention seeking, and manipulation all seem so very clear in this situation now, yet at the time, I honestly saw it more as generosity and caring. The art of masking narcissistic traits to be seen as kindness seems to be one of the narcissist's specialties.

In our conversations over the next few weeks, Kathy let me know that she and Lester were very close, not by telling me straight up but by hinting at examples of how they spent time together, the things they had in common, the places they lived together, etc. She wasn't hateful but rather arrogant and boastful about it.

"My son" this and "Me and my son" that—she hardly ever called Lester by his name when she talked about him. It was "my son" instead of "Lester." I thought it was a language barrier, who knows. I thought maybe in Hungary they just say "my son" a lot. But over time, I realized it was almost certainly not a language barrier kind of thing. I realized it was a typical narcissistic mother kind of thing, indicating that she "owned" him. He is hers, and he does not have a name. It indicates that he is not to have his own persona but is *her* creation. A possessive narcissistic mother will see her son *as hers* and not allow him to have individuality. She would therefore not say "Lester did a great job" or "Did you ask Lester?" It was *her* son that did a great job, and the question would be if I had asked *her* son. This way, even in words, she was *always* connected to him.

There was nothing I could have done differently to be a good daughter-in-law. I knew she hated me for stealing her son from her. All his life, he worshipped only her, and now he had fallen in love with another woman that was going to take her place, and she was not okay with that. Her hate went as far as changing her will one week prior to our first wedding to include the following disclaimer: *"My son's girlfriend Micha is not entitled to any of my personal properties as well as real estate property. Micha is also not able to visit or step foot on my property at [home address]."* In addition, she had Lester quit claim his half of the house to her at that time; she became the sole owner of the house.

Lester said he was aware of it but tried to excuse it as necessary for tax purposes. At least that's what she told him, he said. Later, as she started showing beginning signs of dementia, we changed it back into both of their names.

While I would not talk about my personal affairs to others too much, I would find myself confiding in close friends, seeking answers as to why I felt like my mother-in-law was a bit over the top when it came to acting like she was more special than others. The way she made me feel was belittling since I was usually seen as a strong woman, a fighter, and an accomplisher. It left me confused. In one of these conversations, a friend suggested researching narcissism. I followed my friend's advice, bought books and books, googled, and watched numerous YouTube videos. In the end, I concluded that my mother-in-law fit the image of a narcissist. The way she would put me or others down was the most obvious trait. She'd do things like call other people stupid when they made a mistake or treat waitstaff like they were servants when we went out to eat at a restaurant.

LESTER FELT TORN BETWEEN HIS MOM AND ME

When I married Lester, I knew that I wanted to share the rest of my life with him. And by sharing our lives, I meant sharing the good and the bad, in sickness and in health—just like our wedding vows. When he had his car accident and suffered a severe brain injury, I found myself making the conscious decision that once he woke up, I would be with him regardless of his condition. He could be fine, or he could be in lifelong need of assistance. I was determined to put God first in taking care of my husband. And for a long time, I really thought he was working toward that as well.

A man shall leave his father and his mother and be joined to his wife; and they shall become one flesh.

[GENESIS 2:24]

While he said these vows with me, seemingly full of conviction and out of love, there was a difference. His vows had a different meaning to him. Becoming "one flesh" was not really something he was going to be able to do, as part of his body and soul was already promised to his mom. I am quite convinced that he didn't even realize he was not going to be able to fully let go of his mom simply by saying a few words and putting a ring on his finger.

One of his old friends said to me, "I didn't think he would ever get married—not as long as his mother was alive anyway! You must be quite special to have gotten past her!" I don't think I ever got past her though. Looking back, I did not have a chance to ever be able to be my husband's first lady as his mother had already taken that place in his life.

Over time, it became more and more clear that he felt often torn between his mother and me. Again and again, I just brushed it off, thinking that it took time and that things would get better. There was one time, though, when Kathy made it quite clear to me how she felt about her role in our marriage.

"Just know this," Kathy said.

"When you married my son,

you also married me!"

When she indicated that she was part of our marriage, I asked Lester how he felt about his mother talking to me like that. He brushed it off and told me not to listen to her.

"It's just the way she feels, don't worry about it," he said to explain her behavior.

He even told me I may have a hard time understanding his particularly close relationship with his mother since I grew up without a strong bond to either of my parents. It felt like a subtle hint that maybe I was making things up, that I was jealous of his mom. His mom had made the same claim to me, so maybe I really didn't understand their special bond?

I kept thinking that maybe I was being too possessive, that maybe I just needed to step back and respect the love they had for each other. It was true I didn't grow up with a mom, so maybe I really did just envy them a bit much.

I figured it was I that needed to show more understanding and respect, acknowledge she was there before me, and be resigned to the fact he was just very attached to her. And I didn't want to lose my husband over his mom. She was not going to last forever, but I would be his wife until the end of days. I had endured so much in life; I assumed I would be okay, telling myself the same thing over and over: "It will get better. There will be a day when I will matter more than her. Just give it time."

I remember Kathy telling me the story of Lester's promise after his dad's passing on several occasions, as if she wanted to make sure I knew that Lester would always take care of her. Today, I'm left shaking my head, knowing that with this statement, he had sealed himself into a future with his mom always by his side. He was trapped. And it had become clear that she would do anything in her power to make sure it stayed that way.

One would think, *But he is an adult; he can make choices. He can choose to not let his mom dictate his life.*

And while I must agree with that in most cases, when it comes to emotional abuse, this looks a bit different for the victim. After having a lack of boundaries growing up, the child (now an adult) never develops individuality.

Without individuality, you don't get to make choices like that. You will always be dependent on another person to guide you through decisions. Let me try to explain it with research.

RESEARCH

In an enmeshed relationship, one party may feel like they don't even have a choice but to be enslaved to the other person. Decision-making is never done without wondering what the other may think of it and then finally basing actions on what they think the person would expect from them.

For the mother-enmeshed man specifically, this relationship removes the feeling of individuality and gives him a constant feeling of attachment to his mother. As a result of this enmeshment, there are two main feelings that emerge in the MEM: anger and guilt. The son often finds himself either angry because he feels like he must do what the mother tells him to do, or he feels guilty because he doesn't want to do what the mother tells him to do. These two emotions can leave the MEM feeling trapped, as neither option allows him to feel satisfied with the outcome nor do they give him a feeling of self-worth. The anger can turn into rage, while the guilt can turn into a feeling of shame or betrayal of the mother's wishes.

Due to the fact the MEM lacks a feeling of individuality, he does not even realize that he could stand up for himself and prevent anger or guilt from developing. Being emotionally enmeshed will not allow him to see himself as separate from his mother, and this eventually removes any chance of growing into a separate individual as a result. Over time, his mother's well-being becomes his primary responsibility, and he eventually neglects, ignores, or denies his own needs, wants, and desires. This form of submission to the mother is perceived by the MEM as love and consequently becomes the definition of love in his relationships with other women. In line with this early development follows his undying loyalty to the mother. And while loyalty usually presents itself as a choice, this loyalty is a subconscious response by the MEM but initiated by the mother, creating a lasting and compulsive need for the MEM to remain loyal to his mother.

A wonderful article that I found helps to identify enmeshment trauma and information on how enmeshment impacts relationships. On this site, it differentiates between three different types of enmeshed parents.

The first type, *the romanticized parent*, is mainly the type that Kathy was to Lester. It is that parent that uses the child as a replacement for a spouse. In a mother-son relationship, the son becomes the surrogate husband, which puts a lot of pressure on the child, as it becomes his responsibility to guarantee the mother's well-being and happiness.

Then there is *the helicopter parent* who makes it their mission to protect the child from even the slightest harm. This overprotective behavior leads to the removal of necessary boundaries and limited decision-making abilities.

The third type is a less common but a just as invasive type of parent: *the incapacitated parent*. Instead of seeking assistance from proper institutions, the responsibility of the caregiver is laid upon one of the kids, usually the oldest. The roles of parenting become reversed. A variation of this type includes addicts that leave parenting of an infant up to one of the other children. The consequences are often that those kids grow up to be compulsive caretakers.

For more information, please check out emotionenhancement.com. I highly encourage you to dig deeper into this website regarding enmeshment.

———————

TAKEAWAY

My takeaway about all of this is that I should have set an ultimatum early on with Lester. I should have requested boundaries, made him understand that I was not okay with her being part of our marriage.

So, am I to blame for the consequences?

Should I search for what I did wrong?

At what point should I have done this or that?

Not quite. I have always been a person that feels like I need to fix situations or bend over backward in life to make things work. To hang in there and try my best to make things right with Lester's mother was in my nature. Being an empath and being a person that is empathetic and responds to other people's miserable moments with understanding is my "normal."

Now I know that without realizing I was dealing with a narcissistic person, I was doomed to get hurt. There was nothing I could have done differently or better. Nothing would have ever been good enough or would have changed her ways.

Knowing now what I didn't know before allows me to make better choices—starting with walking away before it ever even gets to anything that would end up in an emotional roller coaster.

If you feel like there should be more distance between your spouse and their mom, you might be right.

If you feel like they put her before you, you might be right.

If you feel jealous and wonder if that's wrong, you might be right.

The parents of your spouse should be respected and honored. If there is a close relationship between your spouse and their parents, then that is okay if boundaries are also being respected and honored by all parties involved.

The parents should respect that you and your spouse live a separate life apart from them and that the parent may not know everything that goes on in your lives.

Your spouse should respect that you as their partner come before their parents. And when it comes to sharing information with the parent, there should be boundaries as to what and how much. Anything that is intimate between you and the spouse should stay there: between you two. The parent should not use techniques to manipulate your spouse. For example, if you have dinner planned and it becomes a regular thing that the parent becomes sick or needs something during that time, there needs to be a talk about the boundaries in place.

What if you are at the very beginning of a relationship with an enmeshed spouse? I strongly suggest you reconsider. A possessive mother-in-law is hard to change—if not impossible in most cases. It almost guarantees issues in the future. If you are not willing to share your spouse at least to a certain point, it may be better to just not go any further with that relationship. No matter the decision you make, it will not be easy.

But if you find yourself already in the middle of a relationship with a possessive mother-in-law, maybe even have years invested into it, I don't promote just walking away, as I do believe in giving the relationship a chance.

Try the following first if you feel there is a good chance for improvement. I found these tips on the *Her View from Home* website in an article called "5 Tips for Dealing with a Toxic Mother-in-Law":

(If you have already tried and tried these suggestions, chances are, you are at the end of your rope. Walk away.)

☑ You don't have to like your mother-in-law or even be friends but remain respectful. Anything she says or does against you is not personal. It's not you. It's her. She will never be okay with their choice in a partner.

☑ Define specific boundaries with your spouse. Talk them out, let your spouse know how close is "too close."

☑ Stop going the extra mile to please the mother-in-law. You can't please her. Stick to necessities and invest time in yourself instead.

☑ Disrespect from the parent toward you is never okay. Fill your spouse in when you feel that the parent has done you wrong. Then confront the mother-in-law, letting her know that disrespect is unacceptable. (The fact that you should also show her respect goes without saying, of course.)

☑ Create distance, either physical or emotional. But also allow reasonable time for your spouse to spend with the parent. I know, that sounds weird, but it works sometimes to give the mother-in-law her "fill.")

☑ Forgive the parent for wrongdoings. Without forgiveness, you wake up angry every morning while they get to wake up without a care in the world. Forgiveness is for your peace, not to take the blame or accept wrong behavior.

If you are already past all this and have walked away but still feel the anger, please do yourself a favor and work on bullet point number six. Work on forgiving your (ex) mother-in-law until you wake up in the morning feeling good, without anger, knowing you are an amazing person that gave your all. It was not your fault, and you did enough—maybe even way more than enough.

I know I am asking a lot from you but learning to forgive is the best lesson I ever learned. It is freeing and delivers happiness into your heart.

———————————

Here are some of my favorite forgiveness quotes from famous people. Enjoy!

"Forgiveness does not change the past, but it does enlarge the future."

−PAUL BOOSE

"The act of forgiveness takes place in our own mind. It really has nothing to do with the other person."

−LOUISE HAY

"Throughout life, people will make you mad, disrespect you, and treat you bad. Let God deal with the things they do, 'cause hate in your heart will consume you too."

−WILL SMITH

"The stupid neither forgive nor forget; the naive forgive and forget; the wise forgive but do not forget."

−THOMAS SZASZ

"Forgiveness isn't approving what happened. It's choosing to rise above it."

−ROBIN SHARMA

"True forgiveness is not an action after the fact. It is an attitude with which you enter each moment."

−DAVID RIDGE

"Forgiveness is a gift you give yourself."

—TONY ROBBINS

"Forgiveness is like faith. You have to keep reviving it."

—MASON COOLEY

"The practice of forgiveness is our most important contribution to the healing of the world."

—MARIANNE WILLIAMSON

"Anger makes you smaller while forgiveness forces you to grow beyond what you were."

—CHÉRIE CARTER-SCOTT

"To forgive is to set a prisoner free and discover that the prisoner was you."

—LEWIS B. SMEDES

"Forgiveness is not an occasional act. It is a constant attitude."

—MARTIN LUTHER KING, JR.

"Letting go doesn't mean that you don't care about someone anymore. It's just realizing that the only person you really have control over is yourself."

—DEBORAH REBER

"As long as you don't forgive, who and whatever it is will occupy a rent-free space in your mind."

—ISABELLE HOLLAND

MOVING FORWARD

I am not here to advocate for you to leave your partner simply because he is a mama's boy. In general, it's okay for a man to have a close relationship with his mother. Unless you find this emotionally draining, chances are they are good husbands even if they ensure their mother's happiness before their own or yours.

What you may wonder is, can the situation be improved? Can your husband change?

If you are determined to stay in your marriage and want to take steps to improve your relationship, know this will take some work. It will also take understanding on your part that your husband may be ignorant to your feelings and unaware that his mother has emotional control over him.

The chances for your situation to improve or for your husband to change are slim. But it is not impossible. For your situation to change, it would be easier for you to make the adjustments within yourself than to ask him to stop or slow down his relationship with his mother. You would need to continue to work on and improve your own ability to tolerate his behavior as well as his parent's behavior. It would also take giving him an opportunity to prioritize you over his mom gradually. By doing so, you would get to work toward a great relationship filled with love and peace for the rest of your days.

* * *

We have come quite far to see the signs and understand the possible consequences of enmeshment between a parent and a child. We received a general understanding about narcissism as the source of some unhealthy relationships, learned the difference of overt and covert narcissism, and discovered the results of a narcissistic mother raising a child. We also learned about a son who was raised to be a surrogate husband and how this can lead to him becoming a mother-enmeshed covert narcissist.

If you have a feeling that your spouse's relationship to his mother is too close, ask yourself:

☑ Are there similar situations that you find yourself in? Or maybe a friend of yours?

☑ Have you been feeling jealous of your mother-in-law?

☑ Does he lie to you and then use his mother as an excuse?

☑ Does he lie and tell you it is because he knew it would upset you?

☑ Do you feel like your mother-in-law knows more about your marriage than you do?

☑ Is your husband repeating things his mother did without "making it his own?"

☑ Do you feel like his first thought is *I wonder how mother feels about that?*

☑ Have there been times when you feel like a third wheel when his mother is present?

☑ Does it feel like you are together "until Mom do us part?"

☑ Does your mother-in-law know things that should be kept between you and your husband only?

☑ Does the thought of wishing she were gone come to mind and make you feel guilty for even thinking something like that?

☑ Do you feel like there should be more boundaries between his mother and your marriage?

If any of these questions sound familiar, then you may be in a relationship with a mother-enmeshed covert narcissist. And if you are not sure, know that this is okay. You now know a little bit more and know what to look for.

Maybe your spouse is simply a good guy that loves to give gifts, spoil you rotten, and has a great relationship with his mom where he does a good job enforcing boundaries. Or maybe you realize he doesn't fit the "MEM profile" where he would put you second after his mom. Let me remind you that not all sweet, mom-loving men are MEMs. As a matter of fact, I truly believe most are genuine and will truly love their spouse in a healthy, loving, and caring way.

I don't blame myself and neither should you for not seeing any of the red flags that my husband might have been the victim of emotional abuse. It is hard to detect and very uncommon for a man to be raised by a narcissistic mother in an enmeshed relationship, and for that man to be a covert narcissist himself.

How was I supposed to know? How is anyone in that situation supposed to know during the onset of this type of a relationship? Everything seemed so very perfect except for a few easily overlooked instances.

I may have said it before, but I want to say it again. Know that everything I write in this book stems from either my own experience and reflects what happened in my life or a piece of information I found online. Please keep in mind that everyone's story is different. This is not a cookie-cutter subject. Every story is different, and there is no single correct answer. I come across many recommendations for people like us to seek expert help—meaning speaking to a counselor—to help determine if you are a victim of emotional abuse. Then you can work through dealing with solutions.

The bottom line is this: When you feel like your mother-in-law is a bit too close to your husband and this causes friction between you and him, you are doing the right thing in asking questions and trying to find answers.

If you are the victim of this type of silent abuse, my hope is to give you more understanding of the cause of it. Keeping in mind that a MEM is also a victim of abuse by his mother but chooses loyalty to his mom over you, I hope you will have a much-needed understanding of your own feelings, reactions, and moments of doubt to allow yourself to move forward into healing and forgiveness. As it happens, forgiveness will be the focus of our next chapter.

"Forgive others not because they deserve forgiveness, but because you deserve peace."

–JONATHAN HUIE

CHAPTER 9

NEW BEGINNINGS

BACKGROUND STORY

FINDING A SUPPORT GROUP

I felt overwhelmed with the emotional attacks from Lester's mother and his friends and all the events that led to our divorce. I never found out why his mother, his friends, and even our best man didn't like me—hated me even. I didn't get an explanation or a reason from any of them directly. Not knowing what I did to deserve such mistreatment left a huge void inside me that I had to work on.

When I began my research for this book, I finally got some answers when I came across the term *flying monkeys*. As per *Psychology Today,*

> Flying monkeys get caught up in a narcissist's plan— often to damage the life of another person. They're often involved in pleading the case of the narcissist. Narcissists love having at least one flying monkey as it makes them feel important. The narcissist often recruits their

flying monkeys from among other family members. Close friends or work colleagues may also become flying monkeys.

This was the best explanation I could find that made sense since not all his friends disliked me. I am still in contact with quite a few that knew about the unhealthy mother-son relationship Lester and Kathy had. Those friends backed me up, supported me, and showed respect in any given situation. With the others, I don't think I ever even stood a chance. What I did notice, though, was the fact that each one of them "worshipped" Kathy. Another common dominator—and the one that I think is most significant—was that these friends *all* (except for the drug dealers) had borrowed or received free money from Kathy over the years. And who knows, maybe that was the reason they worshipped her. I truly believe they all were Kathy's and Lester's flying monkeys.

While I have always been a Christian believer, I never really felt a deep relationship with God. I mentioned before that after Lester's accident in 2015, in the darkest hours of my marriage, I decided to stop by the same non-denominational Christian church I had been passing for years. It was on a Sunday in August that I decided to go inside. My eyes were swollen from crying, my head was hurting from all the emotions, and my body was numb to the world as I walked inside. The sermon was about to begin. I sat in my chair with hundreds of people surrounding me and still felt so alone. Then there was this one song, "I Am Not Alone" (originally by Kari Jobe), presented by what I thought was the voice of an angel, speaking directly to me. In that moment, I knew that things were going to be okay, and that God would dry my tears. A few people sitting in the same row gently wrapped their arms around me and told me that I was in the right place.

After the sermon, I intended to just walk outside, get in my car, and go home, but some ladies stopped me and invited me to come to their weekly women's group. They assured me that I was not alone and that I would find support there.

I went that Tuesday and was welcomed by one of the ladies who'd seen me that past Sunday. She gave me a piece of paper with a poem written on it called "Letter from God" and said, "I was going to give this to someone else, but I believe this is for you."

I started going every week and bonded with some of the ladies. I felt safe and heard. I was broken but learned that I was not alone. I realized they were all broken. They all had some sort of issue, some with their health, others with their children, themselves, or like me, with their husbands.

It was these group sessions that pulled me out of the darkness, and within just weeks, my tears had dried up and I started feeling alive again. While I had retracted from social media, gym time, and anything else I had enjoyed in the past, I began to write social media posts about hope and prayers and finding God and learning to trust in him. I was slowly understanding what it meant to give him all my problems and to totally surrender. The hurt and the pain were simply too much for a person to carry but giving it all to God meant that I had the assurance I'd be okay.

HOW TO FORGIVE

One of the sermons at church was all about the first step to forgiveness. The pastor talked about laying any latent hate and anger at the bottom of the cross. This is to be taken spiritually, not literally. As I mentioned before, the church had a large wooden cross set up just inside the main doors for the purpose of teaching. There were small river rocks surrounding the base, and there were permanent markers lying on a table next to it. We were told to think of one particular person who had hurt us and was holding us back from being happy.

The first person I thought of was Kathy and the pain she had caused over the years. I knew I needed to forgive her in order to start my own healing process. So, I wrote her name on one of the rocks, mumbled some words that I thought of as a prayer, became still for just a moment, and then with great intention, dropped the rock at the bottom of the cross. "I forgive you Kathy," I said out loud. I broke down in tears, feeling every pain she had ever caused me passing out of my body then slowly disappearing. I felt the love of God filling the emptiness that remained inside me. My heart was full, and I could feel the promised comfort and peace flowing through my veins.

So was this it? I put down a rock with her name, and that's it? Forgive and forget? I learned quickly that the pain came back. I realized it would take time again and again to truly forgive. Forgiveness is a skill and needs to be practiced. It comes with trying, falling back, and trying again until there is no more pain within you. It took many months of working through that process to learn how to let go of the anger I had toward her for being so unreasonably hateful. It took many more months to soften my heart and remove all the scar tissue of hardened emotions I'd developed toward her in the first years of my marriage to Lester.

To start my learning process of forgiveness, I followed the example of the movie *War Room* and built out a little walk-in closet where I would literally fight my inner demons, and it worked for me. I had watched that movie right after Lester's car accident together with the ladies from my women's group in church. Throughout the healing process, I had to relive many stories involving her to put them in the past. Just as I was done with one painful episode between us, another memory would appear, and I'd have to work more on forgiving her. I had to forgive her again and again and again until there was no more anger left.

Just a month later I got baptized.

I was ready to embrace my first challenge

as a child of God ...

—Forgiveness—

HOW OFTEN TO FORGIVE

From what I had learned at church, there is no given number on how often you should forgive a person. Instead, it is more of an "until"—until there is no more pain inside you. In the Bible, it talks about forgiveness in Matthew 18:21-22 (NIV):

> 21 Then Peter came to Jesus and asked, "Lord, how many times shall I forgive my brother or sister who sins against me? Up to seven times?"
>
> 22 Jesus answered, "I tell you, not seven times, but seventy-seven times."

These numbers are not to be taken precisely. They simply represent boundlessness, as our father in heaven has already forgiven all our sins. The least we need to do is to forgive each other again and again.

I am mentioning this because even without believing in God, to get over pain, one must forgive the other person one way or another to find inner peace. The process is pretty much the same whether you follow the Bible or not. While I did not want to make my faith the focus of this book, I feel like I do need to mention how my faith (that started as barely existent) grew into a full-blown Jesus-loving-give-it-all-to-him-and-I surrender kind of thing. Without this faith, I don't know how I would have had the strength to move on. I don't know how I would still have my sanity if it hadn't been for God in my life. So I thought I would mention it as a suggestion, something to investigate in case anyone feels trapped in the kind of darkness that I found myself in before I found a true relationship with God.

FORGIVING KATHY

As you know, while Lester was serving time in federal prison, Kathy's disease progressed. I had worked very hard on forgiving her, especially when things got really difficult after the accident. I knew I had to in order to find peace within me.

At first, I visited with her only about once a month, as it would upset her every time she recognized who I was. Then as Kathy got worse, I was able to visit more often since she no longer remembered me and didn't get mad anymore. I actually started to enjoy our visits. We would walk in the small park behind the building, have small conversations, and even have a few laughs together.

Then her health began to decline quite quickly, and she spent the daytime in a wheelchair. I knew the woman I was visiting now wasn't the same one who had once treated me so badly. With the lapse of memory, she seemed freed of the evil spirits that had manipulated her thoughts and actions for the past few decades. As a result, she had returned to a childlike innocence. I learned in this process that even behind a woman who had lived her life filled with hate is just another sister in Christ that deserves to be loved. This lesson was huge for me to understand how to love people that don't love me.

When I had a priest read her last rites in her final days, I prayed with the priest for God to take her home. It was March 14, 2020, when Kathy took her last breath. There she was, finally at peace. I stared at the lifeless body of a woman who had caused so much pain in my last eight years. It was a long road to get here, long and painful years of dealing with her hate for me. Yet I don't regret a moment, as this road led me to fall in love with God, build a quite intimate relationship with my Savior, fight battles that taught me how to protect my heart through forgiveness, and allow me to find peace in the most hurtful situations. The little memorial I set up for her served as a beautiful resting place and reminded me daily that forgiving her was what brought peace into my life.

MY RESEARCH

Now that we've covered forgiveness, it may raise the question of the difference between the type of forgiveness that pardons a narcissist's actions (as you saw in my marriage, I *forgave* my husband plenty of times) and the type of forgiveness that gives you inner peace. Obviously, I had plenty of practice forgiving. I was going back to him again and again, thinking that forgiveness of his lies would help him.

However, despite that I still didn't really have practice with forgiveness. What I had practiced time and again was acceptance, not forgiveness. There is a huge difference between the two. In our interactions, we seemed to use the words "I forgive you" all too often as a way of saying "I accept your bad behavior."

This acceptance is what the silent abuser is aiming for. The victim becomes submissive and is manipulated to think they need to depend on the love and attention of the abuser.

In the world of psychology, I found this "dependency" labeled as *codependency*. I believe it is necessary to know this to break free from the abuser. We need to understand what makes us keep going back, as that was one of my biggest issues that kept me from walking away much sooner.

I love how Lisa A. Romano, one of my favorite online life coaches and best-selling author, puts it on her website:

Codependency is a faulty way of viewing the self as well as the world. The lens that we view life through is tainted, but we don't know it. When we are codependent, we are not independent. As codependents, we tend to attach, and in the attaching to some external relationship, person, or experience. We detach from the self.

She has a huge library of YouTube videos and a variety of online workshops that she offers, as she is an expert in the field of codependent recovery.

She teaches that the way we were raised has a direct connection with the way we act when we become adults. She says, "Children who have grown up in homes that were abrasive, dysfunctional, hostile, emotionally abusive, and alike, are more prone to depression, anxiety, reactivity, and codependency." She further says that we are literally programmed to think and feel a certain way because of the way we were raised. She even wrote a book called *Codependent—Now What? It's Not You—It's Your Programming*, which teaches how to break free from the patterns embedded into our thinking in our early years.

There are different ways this programming can play out. For some, whatever we have been taught in our past is what we see in our life. If you have been taught that you are of little value or that you need to be scared, then you will walk through life with low self-esteem, looking for things that may hurt you. For others, it becomes the opposite. If you have been raised to suppress and deny your emotions, then in adulthood you may find ways to gain control over others or situations that naturally we should not have control over.

I love this quote from her...

"As adults, we owe it to ourselves to awaken from the dream state that codependency is, so we can finally live the authentic lives every human being has the potential to live."

—*LISA A. ROMANO*

———————————

TAKEAWAY

Seeking help from online authors like Debbie Mirza and Lisa A. Romano taught me that I had to change my beliefs.

- I believe I am worthy.
- I believe I am safe.
- I am in control of my thoughts and my actions.

And you need to do the same!

C'mon! Say it out loud!

I believe I am worthy!

I believe I am safe!

*I am in control of my thoughts and
my actions!*

You can find *a lot* of good information about narcissism,
covert narcissism, and online support on different websites.
Following the teachings of professionals like Debbie and Lisa
has helped me immensely to understand that it wasn't my
fault.

I still catch myself falling back into wondering if there was
anything I could have done differently or better. Then I pull
myself quickly out of that as I realize I have done enough—
more than enough—while damaging my own self-esteem by
neglecting my own morals and purpose in life.

I still catch myself wondering if I made the right decision
in leaving the relationship, maybe I should have given it
another try. But again, I catch myself, knowing it was the
right thing to do; it was time to move on. I didn't give up. I
didn't lose hope. Those are evil lies from the devil's advocate
on my shoulder.

Do not listen to the wrong voices. They are negative and
destructive. Know that *you are worthy.*

And yes, I still have flashbacks, hurtful moments that I relive, times when I burst into tears. It has been a lot. It has been traumatizing. And I was wounded, bleeding tears each time the scabs were ripped off by painful memories.

But it is time! It is time to put that behind me. I will not let this define me!

> To be happy, we have to learn to love the self and others, without needing and relying on others' approval, validation, and love.

LISA A. ROMANO

For encouragement or more information about discovery, recovery, and healing, please visit these websites: lisaaromano.com and debbiemirza.com.

_____

MOVING FORWARD

If you are struggling and do not have an answer yet as to how to overcome the challenges that you are facing, I highly encourage you to discover, re-discover, or deepen your beliefs. Maybe not as a Christian necessarily (even though I love being a Christian), but you need a power beyond you, beyond us—something that reaches as far as the universe to have faith in. There is power *in believing* in something that is bigger than us.

And while I have become somewhat of a Jesus junkie, I do not want to push that onto you. I just want to give inspiration as to what it has done for me. There are other ways that I am sure would be good to help you with healing and forgiveness—support groups, for example. All I know is you *will* need support; you *do not* want to try to go this alone. I have listed some helpful links below that will give you a start in your research for answers to the problems in your situation.

My suggestions to you:

- Know you are worthy of love. None of us are perfect for everyone, but we are perfect for someone.
- Fight all negative thinking. Find good in every situation no matter how challenging it may be.
- Understand that with even the best intentions, we all make mistakes, and that's okay.
- Mistakes are necessary to learn how to do better next time. Keep making mistakes, keep getting better.
- Do not allow the past to define your thinking of today. You are in control of your thinking, not your past.
- Take care of your health. It consists of body, mind, and spirit. All three need to be in balance.
- To love and accept yourself for who you are does not equal ignoring ways to improve and grow.

* * *

WE MADE IT!
Well, my dear readers, we did it!

We have reached the end of the last chapter. Only my personal journal and the time line remain. The personal journal entries are what I jotted down after Lester's accident—everything as it happened, notes expressing the feelings that came with the events in the hospital until the time when Kathy stole him away from me.

Fifty-seven thousand words later and I still don't really feel like an author. I am still just a woman who has found a way to share with others in writing how she made it through some tough years in her life. She found out she was on a dead-end road, got directions about how to turn around, and now finds herself heading in the right direction with a clear vision of what's left behind in the rearview mirror.

I hope that my story and my research have given you a basic idea of a few things, including:

You are not alone. The pain and confusion you feel is real. There is such a thing as silent abuse.

But also, that...

There is hope. There is help. You can rise above this. And— you will be okay.

Much love from me to you!
Michaela Bressel

CLOSING PRAYER
Heavenly Father,

I praise you Lord and thank you for allowing me to experience everything in my past that has led me to where I am today. I want to thank you for each and every person that you placed in my life. I understand regardless of whether they did good or bad, they all had a purpose in my life. You placed them there, and I thank you. Thank you for the love that I received from the countless ones that stood by me, loved me, and supported me over the years. But I also thank you for the people that placed challenges in my life, as they too are your children, my brothers and sisters. Through these challenges is how I found you, oh God, and how I learned of your endless love for me. In my darkest days, you were my light, and I thank you Lord.

Lord, I am grateful for the opportunity of coming across a book-writing program that helped me to fulfill my prayer to pay it forward, to do my own research, to jot it down, and to bind it into a book. I also thank you Lord for letting me share what I have learned through a painful experience with others who find themselves as alone as I was, as hurt as I was, and as lost as I was. I pray to you God that this book will help them to find the courage to seek answers to questions that are specific to their situation. Let this book be an inspiration to them, as I know I am not a professional but just a person who shared her story.

I pray Lord that my words will be carried from one friend to another to reach another town and another city and across the lands. I pray that it touches the hearts of thousands of people to help them find peace and love in their hearts and in their lives. May they find forgiveness for those who have hurt them. May they restore what has been broken. May they find their trust again in other people. May they find your love. I pray to you, my God, that from here on they will recognize the signs of emotional abuse and have the courage to walk away from it.

Lord, I also want to pray for those that suffer from narcissistic personality disorder, those with narcissistic traits, and those with other personality disorders. May they too have their eyes opened to the fact they can receive love without abusing others, that they can change. May they find peace within themselves, as they too were victims in the past. May their family members understand them and love them for who they are. May they all find peace.

I pray all this in Jesus' name,

Amen.

MY JOURNAL: "THE ACCIDENT"

Today is Monday, July 27. I decided to keep a journal of every-thing going on with your progress, etc. So, I will backtrack it from Saturday when it all happened. And believe me, lots has happened, and I probably remember it in bits and pieces. It has been pretty rough, so forgive me if I'm jumping back and forth a little. Here we go babes.

SATURDAY—JULY 25, 2015

You left Thursday instead of Friday, and so coming home would be Friday, which of course is terrible on traffic, and it was. You texted me at 11:00 p.m. that you and Kathy would spend the night in Bakersfield with seven hours to go the next morning. Well, four hours, I guess, plus the usual time around Las Vegas.

So at 8:49 a.m., you sent me a text that said, "Good morning my love. Rested and back on the road in Bakersfield, about six hours out. See you soon. Kiss!"

My response, "I love you baby, glad you stopped. 22-hour drive. That's terrible. Tell them no more Thursday leaving." That was at 9:30 a.m.

When I was ready to go to our shop, one last text from you: "Okay baby. See you at home later." Wow. That was the last text at 9:53 a.m. I went to our shop from 10:00 until noon. Then I went to Target, found a dress for my daughter's wedding, bought a few other things, and was debating what else to do on a Saturday afternoon. Well, I had stuff that I couldn't leave in the hot car, so I drove home to see what would come to mind. That was about 3:00 p.m. The phone rang at exactly 3:30 p.m.—a Clark County official number. The guy calling introduced himself as a doctor of the University Medical Center, and after asking who I was to you, he said, "I want you to know that everything is fine. Your husband was in an accident."

Well, I thought he meant last week's wreck and expected him to tell me something about a broken arm. He said, "I don't think you understand. We have him right here. He was in a wreck today and is about to go into surgery. Can you come in?"

My heart dropped. I was being as calm about it as I could. I left; I went to UMC and got there just in time before they took you away for surgery. The doctor on the phone told me, "He walked himself into the hospital and was responsive, but we did a CAT scan, and he needs to go into surgery to drain fluids that are pushing on his brain into the skull."

Okay, so they guided me to where you were. They had already knocked you out. And I got to kiss you and love on you, and then they took you away. Now I went to find out what happened. I thought it happened just prior here in Vegas, but I could not fit it all together. So, my thinking, you must have dropped off your mom, went to Lonnie's. Maybe on your way to drop off the car it happened? That would fit the time line: leave at 9:00 a.m. plus six hours, that would be time to be home. I remember I thought that when I got home after Target you might even be home already.

So next, they gave me your plastic bag of belongings with a pair of shoes and socks and another bag with your shorts, wallet, ID, and phone. I didn't look through it, just took it to the car. They said surgery would be about an hour if everything went well. They also took me into a separate room, and their way of doing that was scary—like official. They handed me a tissue box and told me all the risks of the surgery, which were: 100 % fine and full recovery or any level of brain damage, or in the worst case but definitely possible, death.

After that, I sat in the waiting room. I opened your phone to see if I could find anything that would help me understand, and first thing I saw was that you had contacted Lonnie about a tow truck. So, I called him from your phone. I asked him to tell me what he knew. He didn't respond to that, just asked me, "Where is he the at?" I told him UMC Trauma, and he pretty much hung up on me. Now it was just me and the information on your phone.

Here we go:

11:00 a.m.—You texted him before me that you were back on the road.

12:53 p.m.—You were ten minutes to the I-15.

12:59 p.m.—You talked to Lonnie.

1:03 p.m.—You called AAA.

1:50 p.m.—You asked Lonnie for the address for the tow truck.

1:59 p.m.—You arranged with Lonnie to meet you at Kathy's house. The tow truck had not left yet with the car and Kathy.

2:00 p.m.—You told Lonnie that the helicopter was taking you in.

2:19 p.m.—Lonnie asked for what kind of car and Kathy's number.

No further response from you.

This tells me that Kathy knew something was wrong, and you were taken by helicopter. At this point, I was trying to figure out how all this fit because nobody knew details, and I was in the belief that this all happened right here in Las Vegas.

At maybe 5:15 p.m., Kathy and Maria and her two kids showed up in the waiting room. Later on, my math said that Kathy went more or less straight to UMC with the help of Maria. Of course, the first thing I asked was "What happened?" Well, I started with telling them, "Lester is in surgery, and all that they told me was that Lester was still walking and conscious when you were admitted." Then I asked about what happened. "I need to know since nobody called me the last four or five hours to let me know that he was in a wreck!"

Your mother pointed her finger two inches from my face and was all over me. "You need to be ashamed! You have no rights, you cause nothing but problems, and this would not have happened if you would just leave my son alone! You always get him upset!" I remained calm and just told her "Don't talk to me like that! This kind of talk doesn't belong here! You need to either tell me what happened or get out of my face!"

Great. That was all I needed, a mother-in-law being evil. And yes, just writing about this gets me upset. I was upset, but minutes later, my friends Anabel and Katja came and sat with me for some time while I was waiting for the nurses to call me to come see you. "It will be about an hour," they said when they took you in. Three hours had gone by. So Maria asked the security guy to let your mom to the back. All I know is that without letting me know, Kathy took her badge and walked to the secured area to see you. I was furious. Besides that, I had been waiting nervously but patiently for three hours, and nobody told me to go back there.

Your mother is egocentric enough to just walk back there without letting me know something like, "Hey Micha, we can go see him now!" Well, it was about 6:30 p.m. You had been out of surgery back in the room at 5:30 p.m. Again, I stayed calm. This was killing me. Her being like that. Acting like that. Can she not in a moment like this, get over herself? Well, I sat with you until about 10:00 p.m.

When I went back into the waiting room to let Anabel and Katja know, William's wife, all smiles, told me, "William is on the phone." Of course, I'm confused that they knew. The only one who would have told them would have been your mother; so she called them but not me. This was emotionally almost too much. I was so confused and felt in the dark and left out. Obviously, I'm not part of the family, but Lonnie was? And William and his wife were?

I didn't even exist, and my question for you too was why did you not call me about the accident right when it happened? Just last week, we talked because you had been in a wreck and didn't tell me. "I need to know!" Last week you said, "I knew you were in a meeting, and I didn't want to upset you." Why this time? Lonnie was more important? The money, the stupid job, the car, the tow truck, your mom, but not me? Why didn't you text me?

Right now, it is Monday at 1:30 p.m., and I'm spending my whole day with you as I did yesterday. I have been having so much anger in me about all of this. And there is more to tell from all that happened between then and now. So back to being in the waiting room. Anabel and Katja left and so did your mom and everyone else. I spent the evening in your room until about 10:00 p.m. when I had to go back home. When I got home, I was still upset, still unclear about what had happened, still in the belief that it happened in Las Vegas because your friends, your mother—nobody—would tell me anything. It was terrible. And I couldn't go to sleep.

After some time, I fell asleep in your recliner, but I woke up again from around 3:00 a.m. until 5:00 a.m. Then I slept well. I woke up at 9:00 a.m.

SUNDAY—JULY 26, 2015

So, I got up, showered, got my things together, and went to the hospital. Oh, I forgot. Yesterday evening: Lori and her wife Petra came too. They brought me snacks, and Anabel brought me a jacket, a sandwich, and a blanket because it is freezing in here. It might have been my shock too, my friends said.

It was probably 11:30 a.m. by the time I got to your room. Now my memory gets a little confused, so my time line might be a little wacky. I did leave around 2:00 p.m. to go home and went to the shop to hang up a sign about being closed for a few days.

Well, let's see what else happened yesterday. So your mom gave me a plastic baggie with $2,300 in it, and she told me "I feel like I need to do this. This is from my money so you can pay rent for the shop." Her money? Yeah no. I told her, "It's not your money, it's Lester's money; he worked for it! And he almost died for this dirty money! You don't have money unless you work for it!" It was another moment to test my patience.

Oh, yes. In the morning, I finally got to fill in the big gaps in the time line. I talked to the nurse and asked her what she could tell me about what had happened. All she could tell me was "He did come with a helicopter. We don't have any other information." Then your mother came into the room, and I asked her, "Kathy can you tell us what happened?" With the nurse present, Kathy finally came out with a story. She said, "The accident was around 1:00 p.m., and I don't know where it was, before or after Barstow? I don't remember, but Lester came around the curve on a narrow highway, and there was a rollover accident in the other lane that had just happened. There was no time to brake, and we ran right into it. Then I left with a tow truck that dropped me off at home. That's all I have to say."

So again, I asked, "Why did you not call me from Barstow or while in the tow truck or when you got home?" She said, "Because it was not important. You are not important to me. Lester is, little doggie Keno is, I am important. You? You are not important!" Okay, that was rough. It was right after this that she gave me her money, by the way. Well, if I think of anything else, I will add it to this journal.

By the time I got to your room, they had removed some of the bandages and I was able to see the large incision on your head. I saw it start from the forehead going clear back. You woke up a few times when they lowered the sedation but just long enough to test your reaction factors for sound, voices, pain, etc. They talked to you really loudly and manually helped you open your eyes and move your arms and legs. It all seemed fine. You really got wiggly once you crossed your legs and you just sprawled out. You even attempted to sit up and pull yourself up higher. I loved on you, kissed you all over, and snuggled with you. I closed my eyes with my head on your shoulder and chest and my arm around your body. Your blood pressure was high, but not extreme, but some also the pressure reader in your brain hit the 20, which is maximum, which means no adjustment in the sedation for today. Sleep, sleep, sleep.

William and his wife, Lonnie, Maria, and Kathy were there. I'm being nice—too nice for my standards—but I am not going to feed their gossip with what they want. I am your loving wife, not the enemy that they treat me as. They each came in for a few minutes and left again. They all sit up front in the waiting area; I am not sure why. Talk, talk, talk is more important than being here in the room, I guess. When I near the area, I can tell that they're talking crap because they all go hushed when I am around. I feel lonely. It makes it very hard.

Oh, and one more thing. When I was at home to eat this afternoon and I emptied the bags of belongings, your shorts were cut in half, I guess to remove them from you. But before I tossed them, I checked the pockets. One side had the accident report card from the California Highway Patrol from Barstow. The time of the accident report was 12:36 p.m. So now the I-15 talk started to make sense. You told Lonnie while you were driving that you were ten minutes away from getting on the I-15, so your wreck must have been after Barstow. But the highway is not curvy and bushy there like your mother told the nurse. Now I am back to the thought that keeps coming back in my head: why did you not call me?

And now back to your shorts. In the other pocket was a pack of cigarettes and a lighter. Need I say more? You said you quit! I guess you fooled me with your vape thingies? Ha. I was telling your mother all proud earlier that you don't tell her everything. Bam. Seems I am the one you don't tell everything. I am mad at you. Why do you hide stuff, lie about stuff, and exclude me, and why am I the bad guy to you and your gang?

Here, change of subject. I was asked to assign up to two people to have access to the room between non-visiting hours. So, 6:00–9:00 a.m. and 6:00–9:00 p.m. I only wrote my name down on Friday night. I did that because your mother keeps trying to pull stuff, as if she were the one in charge, and sorry, but I am your wife. She needs to step back. I understand she wants to get information, but the thing is that when she does, she doesn't tell me. So therefore, I set it up so that only I get to make decisions. Good Lord, I should not have to do this.

Why do I have to worry about your mother doing stuff behind my back? And she keeps making others talk for her to the doctors. It pisses me off when William's wife goes and asks nurses or security guys questions.

Here I am getting mad again. I just want to worry about you and not have to worry about them. I am sorry that so much of what this is, is angry stuff. I do not like it either, but it is what it is. This is what I am going through. I can't remember anything right now from Sunday. I know I stayed until 9:30 p.m., and by the time I got home, it was midnight.

Oh, and I forgot. Before I left, they took you off sedation briefly to test you again. You kind of woke up, and I talked to you bunches. You opened your eyes and looked at me. You tried to talk, but that of course didn't work, not with a tube in your mouth. You got pretty wiggly and wanted to get comfortable. Anyway, it feels like I told you this already, who knows. Right now, it is Monday, 6:40 p.m., and I am still catching up with Sunday's report. Let's get to Monday, July 27, shall we?

MONDAY—JULY 27, 2017

The day started better today. I was showered, dressed, and out the door and got to see you before 10:00. They had removed the drain hose out of your brain. Your head was tilted the other way, and oh my gosh, I saw how the incision goes like a horseshoe back to the front above your ear. Now you're really going to have to think of a new hairdo! Haha! I have been posting updates on Facebook. The number of prayers, prayer requests, prayer events, and prayer circles is unbelievable. We have people all over the world thinking of you and praying, which is quite overwhelming really.

It has been quiet today. Your mother stopped by a few times. She is here right now. I always make sure that I share all I know with her—anything about you or your current status. I will not do to her what she does to me. I am nice—not overly but not rude. I am respectful but won't put myself below her. I have been here all day. Danielle stopped by and brought me a coffee from Starbucks. She had asked what I wanted. Well, only my honey really knows. So I took a wild guess on what to order.

Lonnie was here earlier too, and before him sometime a few hours ago, William's wife, but just for a minute. She has nothing to tell you, and it seems to me that she just makes an appearance because she has your mom all wrapped up. Sweet, sweet William's wife—bluh. It won't be long before she will be asking for money. William: yeah, I believe he enjoys being able to visit but not her.

Back to Lonnie: I finally got him to tell me more about the accident. Yesterday after your surgery was his first visit. He came into the room and totally ignored me. I stood up and somehow expected a supportive hug. But no, he didn't even say anything beyond a very silent "Hi." Nothing. But that was yesterday. Today, I learned more about the accident.

So here's what I got from Lonnie today. He said, "I had contacted a friend who rode his bike out to the place where Lester was. That was about ninety miles outside of Las Vegas," so that puts it about thirty miles east of Barstow. "Lester's car had damage on the side and the rear as if he had either switched from the left lane back to the right and then ran into a car, or he was on the left and a car came into the passing lane and ran into his side and back. Either way, there was also damage to the car under the front bumper where it peeled back the underneath plastic and metal toward the back like if he ran over something like a curb. Neither airbag deployed, which I did not understand. I think he was spinning before he came to a stop." So piece by piece, I'm getting the picture.

As I was leaving and turning in my floor pass—only two can be out for your room at any time—the security guy complained that the other lady who had just left—which is your mother— had refused to return the badge. She took her badge home last night. That's against clinic rules, and she just walked out and told them she was keeping hers. What? Again, I am alone to process all of this.

Now back to you. It is almost 8:00 p.m., and I need to leave soon. I want to pick up Keno. He needs to come home. I let your mom have him. Now she says, "No, Keno is staying with me!" Well, she has news coming. I want Keno. He is *our* dog.

Well, that wasn't about you, just more stuff on my plate. You had a bath. Earlier, I had to leave for a little, and they changed the sheets. You had a very calm day today, and I am glad you needed your rest. Rest is good—healing. Your head is less swollen, and you seem more relaxed, and they are working on your digestion. You're not pooping. Hahaha. Well, who wants to voluntary poop in the bed? I get it. And I did tell you about your arm. Yesterday, day two, you pushed yourself off with both arms and passed the pain test on each hand and foot. Today, day three, you passed on all four pain tests, but you didn't react or move your right arm. So they took X-rays to see if the problem was mechanical or neurological.

Tonight, just now actually, at 8:00 p.m., you didn't move your right arm and did not pass the pain test on either hand or foot. So things are getting worse. They will keep an eye on it; they're planning on removing the pressure sensor bolt—as they call it—then trying to lower your sedation. Hopefully, we get to step forward a little baby.

One more thing: Lonnie said that you complained to him— not me thank you—about stomach aches, that you had asked your mother to drive, and that she had refused. Now I know you didn't just ask for the hell of it. Your stomachache must have been bad enough to ask your mom to drive. Was your pain that bad? Again, no word from you to me about that. I feel left out again and again. And I am mad, again. I love you so freaking much, and I get your lies or you're not honest or you don't tell the whole story or others know but I don't. This has to stop. I love you. But if I am not the one you want to share your life with, then why am I here?

Well, I have to go. I am caught up writing in this book, it is 8:15 p.m., you are sound asleep, and I will be back early about 10:00 a.m.

TUESDAY—JULY 28, 2015

It is Tuesday, July 28, 2015. I'm already having a morning. I told your mother two days ago that I would come get Keno. She said again, "No, I will keep him." I said, "No, he needs to come home!" Well, this morning I drove to her house and rang the bell. I saw her and heard her trying to call Keno, but of course he wouldn't come. So she hid in the kitchen. With all the mirrors, I could clearly see her. Keno was all excited to see me. He ran to the back to her then ran to the front to me, back and forth, barking and wagging his tail. I stayed for five minutes, knocked, tapped, rang the bell, called her name, and asked her not to do this. "This is our dog, not yours!" She needs to stop being a bitch. I'm back home, shaking a bit, being upset. Why? After I got back, I tried to call her. But after the phone being busy, she wouldn't answer. I am so tired of dealing with your mother wanting to be an enemy. I am tired.

11:00 a.m. I just got to your room. Coming here was stressful because I fear running into your mother. My heart was beating so hard, and I'm still shaking. I wish things were different; I wish I could focus my mind 100 % on you. Instead,

I have to deal with my emotions caused by her. I know I will confront her about Keno one more time. I know what to say, but I'm praying that I will keep my cool and my manners. I will ask her to surrender Keno, to do it for you, not for me. He is my dog, not hers. She needs to stop being hateful and to do whatever it takes to keep the peace. If she does not return Keno, I will stop asking. I do this with my respect for you, not for her. My focus needs to be on you, not her.

When I got into the room, the nurse told me that your sedation was high. There were two more gentlemen taking measurements of your head for a helmet. A helmet. Wow baby! Stuff is getting real. I want to cry. It is so much to take in, so much to deal with.

A friend from Las Vegas started a fundraiser to help us pay the bills. Your mother gave me $2,300 for the rent for the shop. I needed to pay bills. If she doesn't give me some of your money, then our home life and future is at risk of falling apart. Personally, I'm not scared. I will live in poverty. But is that what she wants for you? Does she not care? I pray that you will still love me and want to share your life with me. We have got to deal with these things sooner or later. Why do I need to worry about this?

I am going to have to ask you to make a decision, more or less, between me and your mother. I cannot take this much longer. My only strength for this stuff arises from my love for you. I love you so much.

I'm back; it is 11:50 a.m. While I was in the waiting room, your mother and William's wife came in, said "Hi," and sat down.

I was texting the girls, so I waved to them and said "Hello." When I finished my text, I turned to your mother and said, "I will be back tomorrow to pick up Keno, and I don't want to bring the authorities with me showing papers that I'm the owner." As soon as I said "authorities," William's wife cut in and said, "Let me tell you about authority!"

I said, "I'm not talking to you."

She said, "Yeah, but I'm here to help Kathy."

I assume Kathy made a phone call after I had left and got her "guard dogs" together: William's wife. Good Lord.

So I finished, calm and mannerly, "I will come over in the morning. Please think of Lester. He may be asleep, but he can feel the tension between us, and you don't have to like me, but you will need to learn to accept me. Lester chose me to be his wife. He loves me, and that is what should matter to you. Your behavior is not helping the situation."

As I finished, William's wife told me, "Micha, you are no longer allowed to come near Kathy's house. There is a restraining order!" All right, it is getting better by the day. I will still try to pick up Keno. This is not right.

So anyway, I am here in the room, and they're not here— or maybe they don't want to be here because I am here. I have been in your room every day from 10:00 or 11:00 in the morning until 9:00 or 10:00 at night. If they cannot get over themselves and come to see you just because I am here, then I think that's low. I don't know why Kathy involved William's wife again. I told you, there is more going on than you know. Your mother prefers that woman over the woman her son loves. Baby, why do I need to deal with all of this?

Okay, back to stuff about you. The doctors had a meeting, and I got to attend. We talked about your blood pressure, which is still high. Right now it is 187 over 108. I told them all I know about your testosterone treatment shots.

I don't even know if you take meds. I don't know your doctor's name. I know some stuff. But here I go getting upset again...

Baby. They asked me about meds. I don't know. Insurance, I don't know. A living will, I don't know. I told them you didn't smoke when you came in; well, I didn't know—I thought you didn't. Do you have a will? I don't know. Who is your doctor? I don't know. *Why don't you ask his mother, she knows everything! He does not tell me anything!* is what went through my mind. So, I don't know. I am only his wife. I need to find my cool—hang on.

I went past the waiting room, and the two of them—Kathy and William's wife—were sitting there. I went to get some water. Once I was around the corner, Kathy rushed to your room. I was there. She said hello to you, patted your hand, and left again. Can she not do anything just out of pure love to you? I will not leave the room just so that she can come in. I'm not stopping her. She chooses not to be with you because I'm in the room. That is selfish. So she is now back in the waiting room. Why is she even here?

See what I mean? I cannot just focus on you. It is messing with my head. I'm gonna get off this journal for a little and check on the girls, customers, emails, Facebook, etc. I will be back, my love.

It is 3:40 p.m. Everyone is gone again, and I have had a rough two hours. I don't even know where to begin. Your mother called me the Devil. "You are the Devil in my son's life!" she said.

People came in. First Kathy—she stayed two minutes, if that long—then Lonnie's wife, Maria. She said to you, "It's all cool man!" You moved your hand, which happened to be toward her, and she looked at me and said, "See, he knows I am here! He is trying to tell me something!" You started tugging on your side like you were trying to move the sheet. When you did that earlier, the nurse said, "It's probably because he doesn't like his catheter."

So, get this. Maria asked me, "Do you think I should grab in there to his you know…his…you know, and maybe adjust it?"

Um, what? I'm standing there, and she asks if she can adjust it?

I said, "You want to adjust it? It is in his dick! You cannot just grab my husband's dick and adjust it!"

I didn't say it very loudly, but I could or should have kicked her in the teeth. But I stayed calm. She blew up and said, "Girl! You are not starting with me now. Don't start that shit with me, man!" I stood there, and she ran out of the room.

Next was Lonnie, and instead of visiting with you, he gave me this big lecture about "We've known Lester for like ten years and only want what is best for him." And he went on and on, making it clear that I know nothing about you, but they do.

Then came a guy I've never met. Another "longtime buddy," I guess. His name is Seth, he smelled like a bar, and he was all loud, talking about how he went 100 miles an hour to rush to the scene. "Man, Lester was fine when I got there!"

Well, whatever. So, sometime later came William. Why does everyone listen to Kathy? Why can they not respect that I'm your wife regardless if they all have known you longer. Who are these people that put me down like I am nothing? Why do I have to endure the pain these people inflict on me?

Why can they not seek peace, just all get along, and not gang up against me? If they are your friends, if they love you, why don't they see that I am a good wife—loyal, faithful, all of that—and I make you happy?

You will not like reading all of this, and I already dread it. Okay, so, anyway…

A Jenny Sparks called me asking about you. She said that a common friend (your mom, I guess) notified her and that she has known you for 20 or more years, which is great. You know I'm fine with that. I'm saying that because everyone here knows you longer and tries to make it clear to me that they care about you–which I do too–a thousand times more! If they love you, I love a thousand times more. If they are worried about you, I am worried about you a thousand times more. Anyway, my mind is all over the place. I am hurting baby. This is not how it should be. Jenny seemed nice. I told her some of my struggles with Kathy and your friends.

I guess she knows Kathy well enough to tell me, "Girl. That woman has pampered Lester for all his life. There is no way she will accept you or any other woman in his life."

Well yeah, I know; I get that.

It is 4:25 p.m., and the nurses are cutting off medications for a moment. Let's see if you wake up. See, that is the highlight of my day: to have been there when you woke up to just wiggle around and cross your feet like when you sit in a recliner. We spent almost thirty minutes together, and now you're back asleep baby. I am I focused and calm. You are my peace. I will just have to work even harder to stay focused and not let other people's issues distract me from my purpose, which is you. By the way, I am prepared and ready to take care of you, no matter what it is that is ahead of us. If you don't get your right arm back, then we will have to figure stuff out as we go. We got this. We're a team baby. Well baby, I'm going home early. Usually I stay until 10:00 p.m., but I need to get some things done at home. Have a good evening and a good night. I will see you in the morning, I love you.

WEDNESDAY—JULY 29, 2015

I got here at about 10:15 a.m., and you were sedated but wiggly and lifted your left leg—not so much your right one, which worries me. They put a sheet on you because you expose yourself to the hallway, but that didn't last long. A few kicks and that sheet was off again, silly guy. But you didn't respond to me talking to you. I was telling you all about my morning. It had been good. I got up at about 6:30 a.m. and had a shake and a coffee or a tea. I don't know; I already forgot—coffee, I think. I went to pay rent for the shop. I was here early but still missed the doctors.

So, here's what I requested. This was not just my idea but a few others' that are not on your mother's side and actually support me. I requested for visitors to be reduced to Kathy and me.

Yesterday was way too stressful with Kathy bringing in all kinds of people. They walk in this room with an attitude, and then I have to listen and emotionally deal with their dislike for me. I cannot have that. My focus needs to be on you baby.

The best I can do is this: upon entry at the front desk, there's a password that I set and share with whomever I want. I made sure your mother has that password, but she knows I requested limited visitors here in the ICU. If she gives the password to anyone else, I will give her one more chance and then remove her from the list. I am sorry that it had to come this far, but they are causing me to be a nervous wreck, and baby, I need to stay strong. I will be the one caring for you for the rest of your life if you don't bounce back to normal.

As of now, anything is possible. They may be your friends, but I am your wife, and I take my place very seriously. It is possible that I may have to get you some crayons to go with your helmet. Of course, I pray for 100 % recovery. But even then, you won't be doing your job anymore. Your job meaning, you know…

You will be released from here at some point. I don't understand your mother. Does she not think about what comes after the hospital? She won't be able to take care of you, and I would not permit it. She needs to get her act together because she will have to communicate with me.

By the way, she is here now, and I am sitting down so she can visit with you, and I can write in my book. It is a lot, but it's all I have with you for now.

Now it is noon. We just got to experience your waking moment. You got quite active but not necessarily good. You wore me out. Legs going everywhere and arms —yes, I said, arms. You even got mad enough that your right arm moved!

It's 12:45 p.m., and your mother just left. Good news: there was no arguing. I let her know that I'm applying for Medicare insurance. I asked about the money from this last trip that you did for our bills. She said that there were problems and that there was only a little money but that if I needed money, I should let her know.

We waited for the doctor together, but after an hour or so, she needed to leave to take care of the rental car. I guess they got it fixed and are bringing it back to the rental place.

The mean nurse told me I cannot eat in here, so while waiting for the doctors, I went up front to get a snack. When I went by Maria, I said, "Kathy will be coming out in just a few." She gave me the talk-to-the-hand gesture and said three times, "Do not talk to me. Do not talk to me. Do not talk to me."

I want to assume that she is still mad from yesterday and not newly mad that she cannot come in, but that is exactly why she is a bitch that cannot just bite her tongue. I do not need that here in the room, and I am not going to leave this room so that she can go and see you without me being able to be nice. She has negative vibes, and I do not want that around you.

Anyway, before Kathy left, I asked to speak to the doctor. He came. We told him that you moved your arm quite well when you were mad enough. So for you to get your breathing tube out, you will have to cooperate. They will lower the sedation but raise your valium. You need to start being calmer and follow commands, mine or the nurses. Please baby, when I say, "Squeeze my hand," do that, and when I say, "Let go of my hand," do that. You need to become calmer.

I know it is hard and you probably have a million questions. I keep telling you that you have been in a car accident and bumped your head, that you had surgery on your head but everything else works fine, that you are tied down and that's why you cannot lift your arms. But I promise everything is fine. All is taken care of. You have nothing to worry about. You just need to stay calm, and everything is going to be all right. It about wore me out the last time you were awake.

Your mom touches you like you are super breakable material, and when you act like this, she's totally helpless. This is another reason why even if she were physically able to take care of you, I just cannot see her promoting you getting better. She would literally pamper you to death. I will have to find out if I can find home care for you if needed when you come home. I will cross that bridge when I get there.

For now, you are here in ICU. It is 1:00 p.m., and you are deep asleep.

2:15 p.m.: I just got back from making a few phone calls, one of them to the Barstow Highway Patrol. I need to send information and $10 to get a report of the accident. Next, insurance. I don't know who your insurance is with. I hope to find out soon and see what the deal is there—not until I get the accident report, though. I don't know how you handled the situation on the scene. Was there a claim made? Were you at fault or the other? I'm waiting for now until I get the report, I guess.

2:20 p.m.: The nurse just reduced your sedation. It's time to wake up a little. We will see how you do. Please behave. It will take for you to remain calm and follow command squeezing and let-go-of-the-hand wishes. Baby, you are moving. I'll be right back.

4:00 p.m.: They increased your calming meds so they can later lower your sedation, so you don't get all frustrated again when you're "too awake." Oh, I forgot; they just told me that you are breathing on your own since 6:00 a.m. It is you who's breathing through the respirator. I love you baby. We're the best team ever.

7:45 p.m.: I just got home and have so much to tell you. I meant to leave at 4:00 p.m. but had a turn in our situation for the worst. Somebody stabbed my tires. When I left the hospital earlier as I was pulling out of the parking spot, I noticed that the Bumblebee was hard to steer. Once I left the garage, I realized something was wrong because she was pulling to the right like crazy. I pulled onto the side of the street to check on the tires.

Sure enough, I had a flat passenger-side front tire. I looked at the other ones, and the driver-side front tire looked low on air as well. I figured I would call AAA to have them put on the donut and I would get the other tire checked at the tire place before I got home.

At the tire place, they checked the flat tire. There was no nail, but instead there was what looked to them like a small crack—maybe half an inch—in the outside wall. They thought it was a crack and not a stab because those are usually bigger and more violent looking. They put on the new tire, then I asked them to check on the other one. They took it off and checked it, and they were surprised to find out that it had the exact same size of crack at about the same area of the sidewall.

Their first reaction was, "Now that is a weird coincidence." They affirmed that it was possible it was from a small pocketknife, but mostly that it was definitely the same size.

What I am saying is this: I believe your friend Maria stabbed my tires. I have no proof, of course. But remember, she got mad yesterday about me looking surprised when she wanted to adjust your junk and got in my face, and then today in the waiting room, she was being hateful.

Well, today Maria also found out that I reduced visitation to Kathy and me and that she was not able to see you. I am sure that that is what pissed her off enough to sabotage my car. I could have wrecked.

When you find this out, you hopefully will know to do the right thing. I am not telling you what to do. But this better not be left with a shoulder shrug. These people are evil and do not belong in our life. I hope you see that. I called the police. I will go in the morning to file a report, then I need to call my insurance to see if vandalism is covered. Who knows.

I also called your mother and told her that I had two tires slashed on my car and I need to pick up your BMW. She said she would pay for the tires.

Well, honestly, my intention is to get the BMW back into our possession—just taking precautions.

She agreed for me to come over and get your car. I called Danielle for a ride, and when we got there, the garage was open and she was waiting. Your friend William's wife was at the house too. No surprise there. Kathy, I am sure, also wanted to make sure I didn't see or get Keno. Why else would William's wife be at your mom's house at 8:30 in the morning? Yes, to stir up more stuff. I am not worried about that as much.

Who I am worried and scared about is Lonnie—or better yet, his wife. She scares me. If she gets mad over little things and slashes my tires, what is next? Slashing my throat?

I'm serious. Anyway, I'm back home. Coming home early didn't happen. It is 9:30 p.m., and I'm finally coming home to sit down. I had a shake and a bag of chips today, and I'm not really hungry. I lost my appetite. I lost weight. I am down to 124 pounds. Good night, my love. You are my life.

THURSDAY—JULY 30, 2015

9:55 a.m.: I got up at 7:00 a.m. Last night I watched a little TV, and went to bed at about 2:00 a.m. I missed you so much last night that I envisioned you standing there walking, talking, brushing your teeth, and all of that. I'm missing you madly. Anyhow, I'm waiting for my turn at the police station to file a report for vandalism on the Porsche.

I did mention to Kathy last night that I believe it was Maria because she was the only one there with her, and Maria just choses to hate me. Maria is literally capable of doing such a hateful thing. God, I just hope that you get this and that you don't just think I'm making stuff up. I hope you don't agree with Kathy and say, "They love me; they would never do anything like this."

I should not have to worry about whose side you will take. I should know that you will know that I would not accuse Maria of doing such an evil thing if I weren't be convinced. It bugs me that I'm worried about if you will get mad at me for accusing your friends. It bugs me that I'm worried about whose side you will take. I should be 100 percent sure.

Right, well, I'm still here at the police waiting, and it is 10:00 a.m.

I love you. Please come home soon.

12:45 p.m.: I'm home but fixing to leave again. The police station filed a tampering-a-vehicle report. I called my insurance: the deductible is $500, and the tires cost $402. So, no penny in our pocket. We only have a few hundred dollars left in our accounts. We're broke.

2:50 p.m.: I am back at the police station. I searched everywhere at home, but I cannot find Keno's ownership papers. Do you know where they are? Did you give them to Kathy? Why do I have the feeling Kathy has all the papers for Keno… Why? Because she has all the papers. She is in control of everything. But I am not calling defeat. I never did go back the next morning to ask for Keno. Instead, I will now file a stolen property report. I have to baby. If Kathy would just work with me…

I sent the $10 and the request for the accident report to the Barstow police department.

Man, I've been driving back and forth since this morning, filing this and that instead of visiting with you. One of the officers just interviewed me about Keno; they will attempt to talk to your mom. The police were on the phone with her. All I heard was a long pause, then the officer said, "I understand that, but…" and I guess she told them she doesn't feel safe for me to come to her house. No problem. So, they sent an officer with me. They're still on the phone—fifteen minutes now. She is doing all she can to convince them of why I should not have my dog.

The officer explained to her that as long as you are not able to make decisions, I take over that position to decide for you, as your wife. So, he asked, "Kathy, if an officer comes with Micha, will you give her the dog?"

She must have said no, and he explained the consequences, like filing a theft report; she could go to jail. She still argued with him. I think she believes that her sob stories will work with everybody. But the law offers no mercy for elders just because they're stubborn.

So, the outcome was that I would go home, call 311 to meet an officer at the gate, and go near the house, and she would give Keno to the officer. She made it clear that I'm not to get close to the house.

Babes, Sergeant Crimson and two ladies at the window witnessed how unreasonable your mother is. Sergeant Crimson called her "a little possessive" and said "Wow!" when he hung up the phone with her. Now if a police officer with experience and people knowledge could not reason with your mother and she wore him out, how am I supposed to communicate with her?

Well, I'm writing this while waiting at the gate. My heart is racing. My hands are shaking. My nerves are about shot.

5:30 p.m.: I am still at the gate waiting for the 311 officer. It has been one and a half hours. What a way to spend my day instead of seeing you just so your mom could get her little ego pleaser that I cannot or should not come to the house. William's wife lied, by the way. There is no restraining order against me—empty threats. That was low.

6:55 p.m.: I have spent three hours waiting at Kathy's gate for the 311 officer just because she doesn't feel safe if I came to the door. I started my period, and I'm cramping like crazy.

By the way, did I mention yet that I am glad I picked up your car because one of the back tires is flat too?

This is crazy! I don't have the money for another tire. I may have $400 in all three accounts. I don't have money to pay bills. I don't have money to go to my daughter's wedding. I feel so lost baby. I am scared. I just want to cry.

7:17 p.m.: I'm still waiting. I called the hospital. Your day was pretty much a repeat of yesterday. I'm sorry I didn't get to come see you.

I called the hospital's number for public safety to see how they can help with those slashed tires. They got nothing. Next, I'm calling the hospital day shift manager to find out if there are cameras at the parking garage. Baby, my troubles are real.

7:40 p.m.: The 311 officer arrived, and I'm staying at the gate while he goes to talk to her. I have prepared a note for her that I need Keno's papers, which I have to assume you gave to her because I searched the whole house and couldn't find them. I also added current bills, totaling over $1,200: Cox Communication, $89.33, Cox Business, $121.91, T-Mobile, $178.81, two tires, $402.06, Health Department, $235.39, and another tire, $301.03

8:23 p.m.: I'm still waiting at the gate for officer to come back. It has been four and a half hours that I have been here.

9 p.m.: I just got home—five hours and no Keno.

She refused to give me the dog. Her reason to the officer was that you told her to take care of the dog. I have to find his papers or produce them to even file a claim. Why do I even have to go through this? I just want Keno home.

Also, she told the officers she would not give me any money to pay the bills. I am so tired and exhausted of all these headaches over your mother, her friends, and all of that. Tomorrow I will have to take care of more legal stuff, like finding out if I can review the tapes from the garage.

Good night, my love. Kiss.

FRIDAY—JULY 31, 2015.

Good morning. It is 6:35 a.m. I have been up since 4:00 a.m. I made a shake and a tea and watched a little TV. Today is another day of taking care of headaches. But first, I'm going to leave and go see you. I need to see you.

Oh my gosh baby, you made my day. You were awake when I came in. You recognized me, and you responded when the doctor asked if you wanted the respirator out; you gave a thumbs up. I love you.

10:30 a.m. and the tube is out. You're doing wonderfully. I left at about 1:00 p.m. to go home and do stuff. Then I removed the now-flat tire from the driver backside of the Bumblebee.

Yep, sure enough, same cut or hole like in the other two tires. This one I'm keeping so you can see how tiny it is. Even the tire guys said, "No way that this is a coincidence. Who are your enemies, girl?"

Well, according to security here at UMC, the only cameras on each floor of the parking garage are by the elevators, so there is no way of showing that Maria did this, but I know, and that is what matters.

I went to see you. You were quite coherent but not as much as this morning. I love you so much. We spent a little time together. Then I just sat there watching you sleep.

And one more—I found Keno's papers in the back of the filing box. Now I can file a stolen property claim against Kathy. But I will let it slide for now; I am tired of dealing with her.

Well baby, it is 8:45 p.m. I would like to be back early again, so I better go home now.

SATURDAY—AUGUST 1, 2015

It is 11:20 p.m. now, and I better get to writing things down. I got up at seven—shake, tea, then I left to come see you. You had just woken up and were very agitated, kicking your feet that were still tied down, tapping and patting your hand on the mattress. As soon as I started talking to you, you calmed down. When the speech therapist came in, you got to chew on a few pieces of ice. It seemed like it was heaven for you. We cracked a few jokes, and you smiled so big. It was amazing. You also swallowed a few spoons of water, which is good.

Anthony called. It took me a moment to realize what he said: "Micha, what's the password?" I was a bit confused, trying to drive in traffic. I asked who it was because he didn't say. With a rather commanding tone of voice, he said, "Micha. This is Anthony. Give me the password so I can get in his room."

I said, "Anthony. Yes, hold up. Let me get out of this traffic! I'm driving! Hang on! Where are you?" He said, "I'm downstairs at the hospital," and he hung up.

What was going on? If he was at the hospital, why was he not letting me know? He was our best man! Why did he talk to me as if he's mad or upset at me? And then it came to me.

When I called him to let him know you were in a wreck, he asked, "Why didn't his mom call me?" I said, "I don't know," and I apologized that I didn't call him sooner. He asked if Kathy was okay; I said yes. While I was telling him how you were, he had no interest in the conversation and said he was going to call Kathy.

So, my theory is that she put crap in his mind too. Maybe I'm paranoid about your mom, but maybe I'm right. Why would

Anthony not let me know that he was coming? I bet he went to your mom's last night to be here this early at the hospital.

Now, the hospital security had asked me to set a new password back when I restricted visitors to enter with password only. And that is the password that your mom has. She should be able to get in.

So, to be clear: I didn't change the password—just in case your mom was revving Anthony up about how evil and uncivil I am and got him to believe I'm acting all hateful. It is not me acting like that; it is her starting stuff with everyone.

And since they all know her better than they know me, I am the black sheep, the evil wife. I really believe Anthony is hating me right now. I texted him to let him know that if there is anything that he needs, he can call me anytime to talk about whatever it is that is bugging him. He responded that everything was fine.

Well, I don't believe him. I think he just will not converse with me and that your mom has everything to do with this. I am trying not to let this get to me too much.

I have you to worry about. I love you baby.

SUNDAY—AUGUST 2, 2015

Good morning. It is Sunday. There is not much news today. You still respond amazingly when I'm there. I told you, "I love you baby," as soon as I came in, and I got so excited when you opened your eyes. You moved your lips so I could read, "I love you too." You closed your mouth and pointed your lips to get a kiss—amazing. I am the happiest girl ever.

You have been running a fever; they're not sure why. So, they started you on antibiotics.

FYI, I have about $150 to our name. Your mother refuses to help. It's okay. She hasn't visited today; I will ask her again when I see her. And you tried to say something. You barely moved your lips, but it was the first time you have tried to converse. I went home around 8:30 p.m. I have to get some rest.

MONDAY—AUGUST 3, 2015

Good morning, my love. I'm back in your room. You're still asleep. The current time line is this: Once you wake up more and become more responsive, they will do the swallow investigation. As of now, you'll spend a couple of weeks here, then in rehab—but only if insurance kicks in. If there's no insurance, then rehab only as much as necessary because it's not anything life threatening. And they will send you home. I want you home. But I have to run the shop to save our business, and your mother is out of the question. She's absolutely not qualified or capable to take care of you—not to be mean. But you're strong, and you're heavy—no way she could do what nurses do.

We will see. I'll try my best to arrange for the safest way possible to take care of you. I love you baby.

I spent most of the day with you. And, of course, how can a day go by without something from Kathy to report? But first, the good stuff—well, stuff about you. They took you off the medication some, but you're still on the relaxer and slept most of the day. I brought your shaving stuff, and I shaved first your upper chest from nipples to upper shoulders so that the sticky monitors would stick better: much better. I got rid of a million pieces of tape that were tangled up in your hair. While I was at it, I gave you a baby-face kind of shave job. You would be so proud of me—not one nick. It took me forever, but we got it done baby. You look so clean-cut again; I love it.

Now to the stuff I don't want to talk about, but it must be said. I had to deal with this crap. I was by your bedside, having been there for hours shaving, talking, checking cleaning, loving, and watching. I had hardly sat down when an unknown woman came walking into the room. She totally ignored my presence, grabbed your hand, and started rubbing and touching you up and down your arm.

She didn't say a word to me but said, "Hi Lester. I'm here now. Everything is going to be all right."

I said, "Excuse me, but I'm his wife. Have we met?"

She said, "I know who you are, and you don't start in on me. I'm here to see Lester. I am an old friend of his—a very old friend. I've known him for a very long time, and I flew here from Hawaii just to see him."

I was still confused. I said, "Would you mind telling me your name and how you know my husband?"

She said, "My name is Vanessa, and I am a friend of Lester and his mother."

I said, "You're the accountant from Hawaii!" I tried to start a conversation, but she remained hostile and gave me a look of hate and disgust. Within ten minutes, she was gone.

You know the way things are. I just don't want accountants to walk into the room and ignore me and treat me like I have done you wrong. If they cared any about you, they would not treat the woman you love like crap like this. I am so tired of your damn mother jacking people who don't know me up against me.

And what kind of friends are William and his wife, Lonnie and Maria, and Anthony to treat me like this? Now Vanessa is next to throw punches at me. If they were true friends, they would trust you enough to know that you are capable of loving a woman worthy of you; they would show me some respect simply because they respect you, but they don't—enough said.

TUESDAY—AUGUST 4, 2015

It is 4:15 p.m. I am home now but had one heck of a day again. Just be prepared. Yes, it is another Kathy story, but let me start with you. I talked to the doctor, and he said that he has to have something that gives me the power to make decisions. I need to get guardianship over you since I don't have power of attorney. See, I told you we needed those for each other just in case. Without it, I have no legal right to make decisions when it comes to medical procedures. I found out that I need to go to family court and file for guardianship.

By 1:00 p.m., I was at the court. First, I had to file for temporary guardianship, which was good for ten days because the regular one takes four to six weeks to get a hearing in front of a judge. This way, there will be an emergency hearing hopefully within a week. There are a lot of papers to fill out; that will keep me busy tonight. I also had to get back to the hospital to get a written certificate from Dr. Shaw that you're currently incapable of making decisions yourself. They got that done really quickly. I was glad.

While I was waiting, I went to your room, and there you were, sitting up halfway with your eyes open. Now that's a first! I started talking about random stuff, and you had tears in your eyes that rolled down your cheeks while you were whispering that you love me. Then you asked, "Where is my cell phone? I want my cell phone" LOL. I wonder what was really on your mind. Why would you want your cell phone?

Well, it's here at home baby. You will get it when you can actually use it. I'm tired and exhausted—emotionally, especially. Now it is time to tell you what happened at noon.

I was talking to you, standing by your side when I looked up and saw your mother. But I was also talking to the nurse who was changing your bed because you had poop all over. Next thing I saw was this blonde gal giving me a big smile. I didn't know who it was. So of course I am friendly. It didn't dawn on me.

Then I saw the accountant girl looking at me evilly while the blonde started talking to me.

"Hi Micha, I'm Lester's friend Jessica. I came from LA to see him."

She was super friendly and smiling. I thought, "Jessica. Jessica. Huh ..." It dawned on me.

I said, "Jessica! Don't you have a weird nickname that Kathy calls you?"

"Yes," she said and laughed. "Yeah, Pookie. I've known Lester for over twenty years. We went to college together!"

First, I offered her a brief visit, as you were asleep and had poop all over—a closed curtain didn't mean anything to them.

So, the accountant was there too and started talking. "Micha, we're here to see Lester."

Then I remembered. I said, "Jessica. You are the girl that about ruined it for us! The one he blocked on Facebook, the one that he told not to ever call him again. Jessica, I need you to leave right now. You're not welcome here!"

Oh my God, freaking Jessica. What is with your freaking mother? I cannot take any more. What else is she going to pull?

I have a million papers to fill out, but she cares more about how to work against me and not *for* you. She wasn't there yesterday, and today she left after five minutes. She never stays.

I shave you, talk to you, encourage you, endure you in pain all while dealing with the legal matters and your mother's behavior. She keeps plotting more crap by calling all her dogs.

She spent so much time against us instead of with you.

Well, I have papers to do. Somebody has to take care of the important stuff. I can't wait to tell her. Maybe she will try to act against me having guardianship. It would not surprise me. I am tired of your mother.

I love you. If I didn't, I would make you choose between your mother and your so-called friends that have zero respect for your wife, and me. But I love you, so I will endure and not make you choose. I will do my best. Anyway, I love you, and I miss you. I am stronger than they think—the hell with them.

TUESDAY—AUGUST 11, 2015

I haven't been on in a while. You were released. We spend time together every day. I checked on the club a few times.

FRIDAY—AUGUST 14, 2015

Friday was a perfect day.

SATURDAY—AUGUST 15, 2015

Saturday was perfect until the afternoon. Lester wanted to meet with his mother. He wanted to ask her to just be a friend, and to stay out of our business though. He said he would just stay a couple of hours. Got no text from him while he was with her.

I texted him; he said Kathy will bring him back in thirty minutes—so after 5:00 p.m.

After five hours, he came home exhausted and fell asleep right away at 9:00 p.m.

SUNDAY—AUGUST 15, 2015

He is emotionally bad—unstable, crying, and scared of me.

MONDAY—AUGUST 16, 2015

He texted and said it was a perfect day. After working at the shop, I went home. He was in pain with the gastric tube. We went to the ER at 3:30 p.m. We got there at 4:00 p.m. There was nothing to be done. We got home at 2:00 a.m. nine hours later. He fell asleep on the couch. I went to bed. It was fine— love, kisses, talk, emotions.

TUESDAY—AUGUST 17, 2015

Lester appeared asleep when I left to go to work, but at work, I checked and saw in our online account that he deleted calls and texts. I went home, and he seemed asleep. I went back to work until three.

In the meantime, I saw that a call came in on his phone from Anthony at 8:30 a.m. Then he made a call to his mom from the house phone. Kathy must have picked him up. I checked his phone history on my computer. He set an alarm at 10:00 a.m. By then, Lester and I were texting stuff about him hiding and lying and deleting everything. I found pics of nude girls erased on his phone. Of course, I was upset, especially about the type of photos.

I came home, and he was gone, and Keno was gone; the computer and all the medications were gone. I called 311 for support to go over to his mother's house. They told me he had already called them and warned them that I would be calling. He did not want to talk to me. The 311 officer talked to him. The officer said, "Lester says that he slept here already last night because you're going through a divorce." I am empty, hurt, and scared. Why would he lie? He was at home last night, not there?

WEDNESDAY—AUGUST 26, 2015

I don't even know where to begin. It seems like so much has happened in just a few days. I've been sending a lot of texts to him. I'm lost and confused, but I realized I need to stop. On Monday, his new attorney called and requested that I sign a paper to relinquish guardianship. He said Lester is a happy, healthy guy and there is no need for me to control his money. The lawyer said we obviously have an incompatible marriage. What the hell?

I looked up narcissism. Lester's mother is a perfect match, and Lester fits the personality of the child of a narcissist.

TIMELINE

AN OVERVIEW OF EVENTS

2007

Lester and Kathy move to Las Vegas

Lester starts working as a local audio installer

2008

Lester and Kathy file bankruptcy

Lester meets Lonnie, a car audio customer, who hooks him up with the drug delivery job

2009

December—Lester starts working in security at a large casino

2012

3 – Soulmates   *August 1*—I move to Las Vegas and start working as wellness coach and later at a sandwich shop

2013

3 – Soulmates   ***January 5*—I first meet Lester**

3 – Soulmates   *January 6*—Lester stops by the sandwich shop

3 – Soulmates   *January 8*—First date (fancy steakhouse); vision board; extravagant circus show

3 – Soulmates   *Mid-January*—Romantic weekend at luxurious Malibu beach hotel

3 – Soulmates   *February 14*—First Valentine's Day; Lester gifts me a Porsche

3 – Soulmates   ***March 1*—We move in together in the rental home**

3 – Soulmates   *April* —Lester sponsors my training for figure competition

3 – Soulmates   *May*—Our flight to my daughter's graduation

3 – Soulmates   *July*—Flight tickets for my kids to visit
us in Las Vegas

3 – Soulmates   *September*—Open wellness club

2014

4 – Wheel of Fortune   *July*—Find out about Lester and
Kathy's drug deliveries

6 – Lies, Lies, And More Lies   Lester's trip to Houston
with his college buddy

3 – Soulmates   **December 27—Get married (for the
first time)**

2015

3 – Soulmates   *January 3*—Seven-day honeymoon
cruise to Belize

3 – Soulmates   *Spring*—Lester quits security job at
casino

5 – Traumatized   ***June 27*—Lester's accident**

5 – Traumatized   *August 12*—Lester gets released from
hospital;
brain damage shows up via immature
behavior

5 – Traumatized *August 15*—Lester's long talk with Kathy; Lester returns apparently scared of me

5 – Traumatized **August 18—Kathy kidnaps Lester;** no communication

5 – Traumatized *September*—I join a local non-denominational church;
find renewed faith in God

5 – Traumatized *September*—Close the wellness club; get job at travel agency call center

5 – Traumatized *September*—Lester starts communication with me;
we start seeing each other again

5 – Traumatized **October—Lester and Kathy go to Hawaii**
Lester "mysteriously" becomes permanently speech impaired

6 – Lies, Lies, And More Lies   I find out Jessica was in Hawaii and that Lester bought her a car

5 – Traumatized *November*—Served divorce papers; we continue to see each other

2016

5 - Traumatized	*January 7*—**Divorce is final;** we continue to see each other
5 - Traumatized	*March*—I move out of our rental home into an apartment
7 - Wash, Rinse, Repeat	*March*—FBI busts into the home of Lester and Kathy; finds $140,000
6 - Lies, Lies, And More Lies	*Fall*—I find out Lester fell on his head in Hawaii a year prior
6 - Lies, Lies, And More Lies	*Fall*—Lester has seizures, lies about driving to see Kathy; I break off our relationship but a love letter from Lester changes my mind after just a few months

2017

6 - Lies, Lies, And More Lies	*February*—Lester proposes to get married again
7 - Wash, Rinse, Repeat	*April 15*—Move in with Lester and Kathy; notice Kathy is "different"

7 – Wash, Rinse, Repeat	*April 28*—Kathy claims I beat her up, and I go to jail; (case was dismissed January of 2018)
7 – Wash, Rinse, Repeat	***April 30*—We get married again**
7 – Wash, Rinse, Repeat	*Summer*—Realize house is under foreclosure; save Lester and Kathy from financial ruin
7 – Wash, Rinse, Repeat	***August*—Kathy goes into a nursing home**
7 – Wash, Rinse, Repeat	*October*—Lester is convicted in court of drug charges; Sentenced for four years

2018

7 – Wash, Rinse, Repeat	***January 9*—Lester goes to prison**

2019

7 – Wash, Rinse, Repeat	***March 14*—Kathy passes away**

2020

7 – Wash, Rinse, Repeat   *March*—I send letter to Federal Bureau of Prisons demanding Lester's early release due to COVID-19; receive notice of his release due to being at high risk

7 – Wash, Rinse, Repeat   *June*—**Lester is released from prison early**

7 – Wash, Rinse, Repeat   *July*—**Lester's "last" lie**; my decision to leave him

7 – Wash, Rinse, Repeat   *September*—My move to North Carolina

7 – Wash, Rinse, Repeat   *October 1*—Lester's house sells

7 – Wash, Rinse, Repeat   *October 15*—**Lester files for our second divorce**

2021

7 – Wash, Rinse, Repeat   *April 22*—**Lester passes away of a heart attack**

ACKNOWLEDGMENTS

—

I'd like to acknowledge those who have supported me by being part of the author community. Their generosity, feedback, and comments have made this book possible:

Shannon Quist (author of *Rose's Locket*) who introduced me to the book writing program by Creator Institute, Alexandra Tebeck, Jan Burgard-Moore, Mario Singh Leyva, Kim Brown, Joni Ana Baes Paez, C. Leavel RN, Brie Bushaw, Becky Childers, Cortney Davidson, Jeanine Narciso, Patsy Pruitt, Melinda Cramer, Deonna Eberhardt-Livandovskiy, Eric Koester, Jennifer Karst, Serena Spescia, Angela Hardy, Julia Arnold, Elli Waldrop, Pat Landis, James Aaron Chartier-Rouette, Shelley Hulsey, Melissa Sorensen, Heather Dumcum, Marie Rezendes, Anna Zubek, Patrick and Ashley Luna, Cody Greeley, Katrina Deslatte Johnson, Sandra Lewis, Candace Graham, Steve Lankfer, Juvencio Castro, Diane Peritz, Angel Marks-Denning, Evelyne Coradin, Terry Peak, Sandi O'Dell McGarraugh, Troy Brown, Julia Breitman, Kim Sampson, Alina Spescia, Debbie Gold, June Jensen, Erin Wilson Smith, Sally Anderson, Cyndi Bollinger, Niki Sandelin, Hellene Alabi-Williams, Keith James, Jeffrey Moore, and Bob Burnett

I'd be remiss if I didn't gratefully acknowledge my super beta readers for putting in a lot of extra effort:
Alina Spescia, Kim Sampson, Becky Childers, and Mario Singh Leyva

I'd also like to say thank you to the whole team of Creator Institute and New Degree Press, including:
Eric Koester (founder of Creator Institute), Lyn Solares (lead teaching assistant), Haley Newlin (NDP coach), and John Saunders (NDP coach)
Development Team: Jesse Rivas (editor), Andrea Miller Hayes (coordinator), Sherman Morrison (wrangler), and ChandaElaine Spurlock (manager)
Publishing Team: Brian Bies (editor, coach), Heather Gomez (pre-launching marketing), and Jamie T. (coordinator)
Video Production Team: Natalie Bailey (coordinator) and Erica Fyffe (assistant)
Acquisition Team: Venus Bradley (head editor) and Rob Neill (editor)
Marketing and Revision Team: Kristy Carter (wrangler), Leila Summers (manager), Annie Taber (copy editor), Amanda Brown, and Kayla LeFevre
Special thanks to Bianca Myrtil (editor) who guided me through the hardest and longest part of the making of this book.
Layout Design: Natalya Belova (senior layout designer)
Cover Design Team: Gjorgji Pejkovski, Nikola Tikoski, and Tea Jagodic
And all proofreaders, layout editors, and all others involved in the final publishing phase

A heartfelt thank you to my children who have stood by my side and supported me through love and patience and to all my family and friends that have stuck with me for all these years, that have lifted me up, let me cry on their shoulders, and given me words of wisdom and encouragement. I love you all.

Lastly, I thank God for giving me strength and guiding me every day of my life. I give him all the glory for the development of this book. May this creation touch countless souls that need love and healing. Amen.

APPENDIX

———

CHAPTER 1

American Psychiatric Association. *Alternative DSM-5 Model for Personality Disorders.* Fifth Edition. Washington, DC: American Psychiatric Publishing, Inc; 2013. 761-81.

American Psychiatric Association. "What Are the DSM-5 Diagnostic Criteria for Narcissistic Personality Disorder (NPD)?" Updated May 16, 2018. *https://www.medscape.com/answers/1519417-101773/what-are-the-dsm-5-diagnostic-criteria-for-narcissistic-personality-disorder-npd.*

American Psychological Association. "Wink, Paul. Two Faces of Narcissism." Accessed June 18, 2021. *https://doi.org/10.1037/0022-3514.61.4.590.*

Britannica. "Narcissism. Definitions, Origins, Pathology, Behavior, Traits & Facts." Accessed June 18, 2021. *https://britannica.com/science/narcissism.*

en.google-info.org. "Cephissus Mythology." Accessed May 15, 2021. *https://en.google-info.org/34773599/1/cephissus-mythology.html.*

GreekMythology.com. "Myths/Mortals/Narcissus." Accessed May 14, 2021. *https://www.greekmythology.com/Myths/Mortals/Narcissus/narcissus.html.*

Interesting Literature. "A Summary and Analysis of the Echo and Narcissus Myth." Accessed May 15, 2021. *https://interestingliterature.com/2020/12/narcissus-myth-story-echo-summary-analysis/.*

Mayo Clinic. "Narcissistic Personality Disorder/Symptoms & Causes." Accessed May 15, 2021. *https://www.mayoclinic.org/diseases-conditions/narcissistic-personality-disorder/symptoms-causes/syc-20366662).*

MedScape. "What Are the DSM-5 Diagnostic Criteria for Narcissistic Personality Disorder (NPD)." Updated May 16, 2018. *https://www.medscape.com/answers/1519417-101773/what-are-the-dsm-5-diagnostic-criteria-for-narcissistic-personality-disorder-npd.*

Mirza, Debbie. *The Covert Passive Aggressive Narcissist: Recognizing the Traits and Finding Healing After Hidden Emotional and Psychological Abuse.* Read by Debbie Mirza. Publisher: Debbie Mirza Coaching LLC. Unabridged Audiobook ed., 6 hrs and 42 mins.

Narcissistic Abuse Support. "20 Covert Narcissist Red Flags by Debbie Mirza." Accessed June 4, 2021. *https://narcissistabusesupport.com/wp-content/uploads/2018/12/20-COVERT-NARCISSIST-RED-FLAGS-by-Debbie-Mirza.pdf.*

National Library of Medicine. "The Five-Factor Narcissism Inventory (FFNI)." Accessed May 15, 2021. *https://pubmed.ncbi.nlm.nih.gov/23647044/.*

National Library of Medicine. "Two Faces of Narcissism." Accessed May 15, 2021. *https://pubmed.ncbi.nlm.nih.gov/1960651/.*

Psychology Today. "What's the Single Greatest Danger of Covert Narcissism?" Accessed May 15, 2021. *https://www.psychology-today.com/us/blog/romance-redux/201712/what-s-the-single-greatest-danger-covert-narcissism.*

Runge, Björn, dir. *The Wife.* Directed by Silver Reel; Meta Film London; Anonymous Content; Tempo Productions; Embankment Films; Creative Scotland; Spark Film and Television; Film i Väst. 2017.

Verywell Mind. "How to Recognize Someone with Covert Narcissism." Updated July 27, 2020. *https://www.verywellmind.com/understanding-the-covert-narcissist-4584587.*

Wink, Paul. Two Faces of Narcissism. *Journal of Personality and Social Psychology, 61*(4), 590–597, 1991.

CHAPTER 2

Adams, K. M. *When He's Married to Mom: How to Help Mother-Enmeshed Men Open Their Hearts to True Love and Commitment.* New York, NY: Touchstone Books, 2007.

Adams, K. M. *Silently Seduced: When Parents Make Their Children Partners.* Deerfield Beach, FL: HCI Books, 2011.

Amazon. *Narcissist and the Peter Pan Syndrome: Emotionally Unavailable and Emotionally Immature Men: Transcend Mediocrity, Book 83;* (Audible Audio Edition): J.B. Snow, Sorrel Brigman, JB Snow Publishing: Unabridged Audiobook ed., 21 mins.

American Psychological Association. "Çimşir, E., & Akdoğan, R. Childhood Emotional Incest Scale (CEIS): Development, Validation, Cross-Validation, and Reliability." Accessed June 18, 2021. *https://doi.org/10.1037/cou0000439.*

Çimşir, E., & Akdoğan, R. Childhood Emotional Incest Scale (CEIS): Development, validation, cross-validation, and reliability. *Journal of Counseling Psychology, 68*(1), 98–111., 2021.

Emotion Enhancement. "How Enmeshment in Childhood Leads to Fear of Relationships and Avoidant Attachment in Men." Accessed 05/24/2021. *https://www.emotionenhancement.com/single-post/understanding-men-how-enmeshment-trauma-leads-to-a-fear-of-relationships-and-avoidant-attachment-in.*

Kenneth M. Adams and Associates, P.C. "Dr. Kenneth M. Adams." Accessed May 15, 2021. *https://www.overcomingenmeshment.com/books/when-hes-married-to-mom/.*

Kenneth M. Adams and Associates, P.C. "Dr. Kenneth M. Adams." Accessed May 15, 2021. *https://www.sexualhealth-addiction.com/about-us/dr-kenneth-adams/.*

CHAPTER 3

Cosmopolitan. "Here's Everything You Need to Know about Love Bombing and Why It's So Dangerous." Written by Lauren L'Amie and Taylor Andrews. Published March 31, 2021. *https://www.cosmopolitan.com/sex-love/a26988344/love-bombing-signs-definition/.*

KidsInTheHouse. "The Different Masks of Narcissism." Accessed June 10, 2021. *https://www.kidsinthehouse.com/all-parents/family-life/the-different-masks-of-narcissism.*

Psychology Today. "The Danger of Manipulative Love-Bombing in a Relationship." Accessed June 7, 2021. *https://www.psychologytoday.com/us/blog/reading-between-the-headlines/201703/the-danger-manipulative-love-bombing-in-relationship.*

The Minds Journal. "How to Identify a Love Bomber: The Narcissist's Soulmate Scam." Accessed: June 7, 2021. *https://themindsjournal.com/identifying-a-love-bomber/.*

CHAPTER 4

Bible Money Matters. "Bible Verses about Money: What Does the Bible Have to Say about Our Financial Lives?" Accessed May 24, 2021. *https://www.biblemoneymatters.com/bible-verses-about-money-what-does-the-bible-have-to-say-about-our-financial-lives/.*

Sam Vaknin. "The Narcissist's Relationship with Money." Published March 24, 2015. *https://www.linkedin.com/pulse/narcissists-relationship-money-sam-vaknin/.*

CHAPTER 5

HELPGUIDEORG INTERNATIONAL. "PTSD & Trauma/ Emotional and Psychological Trauma." Accessed May 14, 2021. *https://www.helpguide.org/articles/ptsd-trauma/coping-with-emotional-and-psychological-trauma.htm.*

Medical News Today. "What Is Trauma? What to Know." Accessed May 14, 2021. *https://www.medicalnewstoday.com/articles/trauma#definition.*

National Center for Biotechnology Information, US National Library of Medicine National Institutes of Health. Introduction. Accessed May 14, 2021. *https://www.ncbi.nlm.nih.gov/pmc/articles/PMC5747539/.*

Psychology Today. "Trauma. What Is Trauma?" Accessed June 17, 2021. *https://www.psychologytoday.com/us/basics/trauma.*

CHAPTER 6

Merriam-Webster. Online ed., s.v. "Definition of Lie." Accessed June 02, 2021. *https://www.merriam-webster.com/dictionary/lie.*

Psychology Today. "The Narcissist and His Lies: How They're Different. The Psychology of Deception and the Narcissist's Skillful Mirages." Posted August 22, 2018. *https://www.psychologytoday.com/us/blog/tech-support/201808/the-narcissist-and-his-lies-how-theyre-different.*

CHAPTER 8

Emotion Enhancement. "Enmeshment Trauma, If Your Parents' Needs Took Priority and How This Impacts Your Relationships." Published February 4, 2017. *https://www.emotionenhancement.com/single-post/enmeshment-trauma-and-how-it-impacts-your-relationships.*

Her View from Home. "5 Tips for Dealing with a Toxic Mother-in-Law." Accessed May 30, 2021. *https://herviewfromhome.com/5-tips-for-dealing-with-a-toxic-mother-in-law.*

Post Wedding Life. "What to Do When Your Husband Is Too Close to His Mom." Accessed May 15, 2021. *https://postweddinglife.com/what-to-do-your-husband-is-too-close-to-his-mom.*

Psychology Today. "The Narcissistic Family Legacy. How Narcissism Can Be Passed Down through the Generations." Posted May 2, 2020. *https://www.psychologytoday.com/us/blog/women-autism-spectrum-disorder/202005/the-narcissistic-family-legacy.*

CHAPTER 9

Psychology Today. "Are You a Narcissist's Flying Monkey?" Posted October 7, 2020. *https://www.psychologytoday.com/us/blog/*

women-autism-spectrum-disorder/202010/are-you-narcissists-flying-monkey.

Romano, Lisa A. "Lisa A. Romano Breakthrough Life Coach and Best Selling Author." Accessed May 15, 2021. *https://lisaaromano.com.*

Made in United States
Orlando, FL
07 May 2023

32906084R00139